Research Skills
for Social Work

Research Skills
for Social Work

ANDREW WHITTAKER

Series Editors: Jonathan Parker and Greta Bradley

LearningMatters

First published in 2009 by Learning Matters Ltd

British Library Cataloguing in Publication Data
A CIP record for this book is available from the British Library

ISBN 978 1 84445 179 1

Cover design by Code 5 Design Associates Ltd
Project management by Deer Park Productions, Tavistock
Typeset by PDQ Typesetting Ltd, Newcastle-under-Lyme
Printed and bound in Great Britain by Bell & Bain Ltd, Glasgow

Learning Matters Ltd
33 Southernhay East
Exeter EX1 1NX
Tel: 01392 215560
info@learningmatters.co.uk
www.learningmatters.co.uk

Mixed Sources
Product group from well-managed
forests and other controlled sources
www.fsc.org Cert no. TT-COC-002769
© 1996 Forest Stewardship Council
FSC

Contents

Acknowledgements

I have had many friends and colleagues who have patiently read through earlier drafts and offered invaluable suggestions, including Martyn Higgins, Lucy Popescu, Tirion Havard, Iain Campbell-King, Andrea Colquhoun, Keith Popple, Lynn McDonald and Donald Forrester. Many of the strengths of the book are due to their diligent readings and thought-provoking comments, while its limitations are mine alone. As well as those already named, I would like to thank my colleagues within the LSBU social work team who have been supportive while I have been rather preoccupied, including Annabel Goodyer, Mary Saunders, John Macdonough, Tom Wilks, Louise O'Connor, Alison Higgs, Trish Hafford Letchfield, Baljit Soroya, Claire Felix, Care Chandra, Wijaya Mallikaaratchi, Jo Rawles, Ruth Watson, Liz Green, Livia Horsham and Alison Chojna. I would like to thank current and past BA and MSc students for their helpful comments and suggestions. I have appreciated the support of staff at Learning Matters, particularly Di Page, Kate Lodge, Luke Block and series editor Jonathan Parker who have been very helpful and encouraging.

A number of key people have inspired me during my career in practice, namely Nick Thurlow Brown, Heather Castillo and Sue Lancaster. They have shown me what excellent social work practice truly can achieve. Since my joining academia, Sue White, Lynn McDonald, Donald Forrester and David Shemmings have provided guidance and inspiration and shown me what can be achieved through excellent social work research and education.

I would like to thank my mother, father and sister Sally and her family, Joe, Lauren-Kate and Ben, for their constant encouragement. I would like to thank my stepdaughters, Samantha and Rebecca, who have looked on with patient bemusement at my constant trips to the British Library. But most of all, I would like to thank Christina, whose love and support have made my life full and rich and to whom I owe so much.

Introduction

This book is written for student social workers who are developing the knowledge and skills to complete the research component of their course. While it is primarily aimed at students in their final year or level of study on an undergraduate degree, it will also be useful for students on postgraduate qualifying courses who have a research component. The book will also appeal to people considering a career in social work or social care but not yet studying for a social work degree. It will assist students undertaking a range of social and health care courses in further education. Nurses, occupational therapists and other health and social care professionals will be able to gain an insight into the new requirements demanded of social workers. Experienced and qualified social workers, especially those undertaking post-qualifying training, will also be able to use this book for consultation, teaching and revision and to gain an insight into the expectations raised by the qualifying degree in social work.

Requirements for social work education

Social work education has undergone a major transformation to ensure that qualified social workers are educated to honours degree level and develop knowledge, skills and values which are common and shared. A vision for social work operating in complex human situations has been adopted. This is reflected in the following definition from the International Association of Schools of Social Work and International Federation of Social Workers (2001):

> The social work profession promotes social change, problem solving in human relationships and the empowerment and liberation of people to enhance well-being.

> Utilising theories of human behaviour and social systems, social work intervenes at the points where people interact with their environments.

> Principles of human rights and social justice are fundamental to social work.

While there is a great deal packed into this short and pithy definition it encapsulates the notion that social work concerns individual people and wider society. Social workers practise with people who are vulnerable, who are struggling in some way to participate fully in society. Social workers walk that tightrope between the marginalised individual and the social and political environment that may have contributed to their marginalisation.

Social workers need to be highly skilled and knowledgeable to work effectively in this context. The then Minister for Health, Jacqui Smith, showed a commitment for social work education and practice to improve. In order to improve the quality of both these aspects of professional social work, it is crucial that you, as a student social worker, develop a rigorous grounding in and understanding of theories and models for social work. Such knowledge helps social workers to know what to do, when to do it and how to do it, while recognising that social work is a complex activity with no absolute 'rights' and 'wrongs' of practice for each situation. We also concur with the Minister in championing the practical application of research to inform social work practice:

> *Social work is a very practical job. It is about protecting people and changing their lives, not about being able to give a fluent and theoretical explanation of why they got into difficulties in the first place. New degree courses must ensure that theory and research directly informs and supports practice.*

(Jacqui Smith, 2002)

This practical emphasis can be mistaken as a call for 'common sense' rather than 'book knowledge'. However, common sense can be used to justify a range of taken for granted assumptions that are often unspoken and may even be discriminatory. Instead, we argue for an approach which is practical in focus but which integrates the best of research findings and theoretical knowledge so we can be as effective as possible in our practice.

The book aims to meet the learning needs outlined in the Department of Health's prescribed curriculum for the social work degree, incorporating the necessary knowledge, skills and the development of values. It also aims to meet the subject skills identified in the updated Quality Assurance Agency academic benchmark criteria for social work (QAA, 2008). These provide the academic standards for the social work degree and specify that your studies should prepare you to:

- be able to critically apply research knowledge to inform your understanding and to sustain and develop your practice (4.2, 5.8, 7.3);

- acquire the habits of critical reflection and self-evaluation and use research findings appropriately to inform your decision-making and evaluation of outcomes (4.7);

- be able to understand research-based concepts, including the status of particular bodies of knowledge and how they can be applied to practice (5.1.4);

- develop your knowledge and critical appraisal of relevant social research methodologies and the evidence base for social work (5.1.4);

- demonstrate knowledge of key research skills, such as statistical techniques, which enable you to effectively use research in your practice (5.9).

In essence, the book will concentrate on supporting you to develop the core skills required to complete the research component of your degree. An action-oriented approach helps to facilitate evaluation and review of your practice. Case studies, reflecting a range of different practice settings, will be used throughout to enhance this process and to illustrate key points.

Book structure

The book has eight main chapters covering every stage of the process, from selecting your topic and writing your literature review through to collecting and analysing your data. In the first chapter you will be introduced to the skills and knowledge necessary to plan effectively for your project. The central distinction between qualitative and quantitative approaches will be explored and illustrated using case studies. Key research terms used will be explained and you will be invited to develop your overall research questions using a concept map. The use of a research journal to enable you to record your progress and promote reflexivity will be explored. The chapter will conclude by examining a range of different research designs and traditions and further reading will be suggested.

Chapter 2 concerns the next stage, undertaking your literature review. You will have had some thoughts about your research topic and are starting to formulate your research question. A literature review enables you to establish what is already known about your research topic. This chapter aims to guide you through that process, using case studies and activities to illustrate the different stages. Various sources and forms of literature will be outlined and common difficulties will be discussed. You will be invited to review specific techniques for identifying appropriate literature and making effective notes. The chapter will conclude with guidance about how to evaluate research studies and different formats for writing up your literature review.

Chapters 3 to 6 introduce you to the four most popular research methods, namely interviews, focus groups, questionnaires and documentary analysis. In Chapter 3 you will be introduced to the different types of interview used in the social sciences. You will be asked to consider the advantages and disadvantages of interviews and when it would be most appropriate to use them. Here you will learn about the range of sampling strategies and their strengths and limitations. You will also learn useful skills to enable you to develop interview questions and design an interview schedule. Practical issues raised by using interviews will be emphasised through a case study and student-centred activities.

Chapter 4 will introduce you to focus groups as an effective and increasingly popular research method. You will explore practical issues around choosing and recruiting different types of sample. The process of developing a discussion guide will be examined and you will be invited to consider different forms of question. Case studies will be used to illustrate and you will be invited to consider different options for recording and transcribing.

Chapter 5 will consider the use of questionnaires as a research method. The distinction between questionnaires and surveys will be explored and different forms of data collection will be outlined. The chapter aims to address the key issues in questionnaire design and to enable you to understand the process and avoid the main pitfalls. A five-stage model will be outlined, taking you from formulating your research question through to analysing your data. You will be invited to consider a range of ethical issues and sampling strategies and the strengths and limitations of questionnaires will be explored. Case studies and practical guidance will be provided throughout to help you manage your questionnaire project.

In Chapter 6 you will explore how documentary analysis can be used as an effective tool in understanding a range of texts, ranging from client notes to government policy documents. Documents are central to the everyday realities of working in the health and social care field and can provide a rich source of data. This chapter will help you to develop your understanding of the stages of a documentary analysis and avoid the most common pitfalls. It will focus on one particular approach, content analysis, which provides a straightforward method for analysing texts. A case study and exercises will be used to illustrate the process.

In Chapter 7 you will be introduced to the practical process of analysing your data. Data analysis is the process of making sense of the information you have collected and searching for what lies below the surface content. While the previous chapters have focused on how you will design your research project and obtain your data, this chapter will help you grasp how to understand the often complex story that your data tell. You will be invited to draw parallels between the skills that you have already developed to understand the accounts that service users tell you and the skills used in data analysis. The chapter will address both qualitative and quantitative data and finish by exploring some of the most common errors made in this process.

The eighth chapter concerns the final stage of the process, writing up your research project. Common anxieties concerning the writing process will be explored and practical strategies to address writing barriers will be discussed. You will be encouraged to consider how to structure your dissertation and common formats will be discussed. Detailed guidance will be given on how to structure the different elements of your dissertation. You will consider how to present both qualitative and quantitative research findings and case studies will be used to illustrate the process.

Concluding remarks will be offered at the end of the book. At this stage you will be invited to review your learning and consider how you may take it forward in the future. Current developments in government thinking on the status and training of social workers will be explored and the importance of post-qualifying study will be discussed.

Learning features

The book is interactive. You are encouraged to work through the book as an active participant, taking responsibility for your learning, in order to increase your knowledge, understanding and ability to apply this learning to practice.

Case studies throughout the book will help you to examine theories and models for social work practice. We have devised activities that require you to reflect on experiences, situations and events and help you to review and summarise learning undertaken. In this way your knowledge will become deeply embedded as part of your development. When you come to practise learning in an agency the work and reflection undertaken here will help you to improve and hone your skills and knowledge.

This book will introduce knowledge and learning activities for you as a student social worker concerning the central processes relating to research in all areas of the discipline. Suggestions for further reading will be made at the end of each chapter.

Transferable skills

Completing your research project will provide you with the following range of transferable skills:

- project management skills, from first conception through to completed dissertation – this includes time management and planning skills as well as evaluation and implementation skills;

- the ability to find and critically evaluate research studies rather than accepting them at face value – this can lead to increased confidence to question your own practice and the practice of others;

- the ability to think and study independently and take responsibility for your own learning as an autonomous practitioner – this can lead to increased curiosity and openness to new ideas.

These are all essential skills that you will use that will increase your employability and positively improve your practice.

Professional development and reflective practice

Great emphasis is placed on developing skills of reflection about, in and on practice. This has developed over many years in social work. It is important also that you reflect prior to practice, if indeed this is your goal. This book will assist you in developing a questioning approach that looks in a critical way at how you approach the research task and seeks to heighten your skills in refining your practice as a result of these deliberations. Reflection is central to good social work practice, but only if action results from that reflection.

Reflecting about, in and on your practice is not only important during your education to become a social worker; it is considered key to continued professional development. As we move to a profession that acknowledges life-long learning as a way of keeping up to date, ensuring that research informs practice and in honing skills and values for practice, it is important to begin the process at the outset of your development. The importance of professional development is clearly shown by its inclusion in the National Occupational Standards and reflected in the General Social Care Council (GSCC) Code of Practice for Employees.

Chapter 1
Planning your research

Introduction

You are about to embark upon a process that is likely to change the way you think. You will gain tools for challenging your own thinking and the thinking of others and get a glimpse 'behind the scenes' at how knowledge is created. As a result, you are likely to experience more freedom than with any other part of the course to intensively study something that is interesting to you.

Historically, social work has seen itself as a 'practical' subject and has drawn upon other disciplines to provide a research base to inform its interventions. Sociology and psychology have been the disciplines that have been the most influential, both of which have relatively well established research bases. As social work has become a graduate profession, there has been a shift towards the discipline developing its own research base.

Developing research skills is an important part of qualifying social work programmes, which usually occurs in the final phase of the course. By this stage in your degree, you will have become accustomed to both traditional academic writing and competence-based assessments such as placement portfolios. However, the prospect of learning a new vocabulary and set of skills can be a little daunting. For example, although all students must demonstrate numerical proficiency before being accepted on the course, this may not translate into confidence in critically appraising statistical information. Even the language of research design, methodology and data analysis can seem technical and remote from students' experiences.

ACTIVITY 1.1

Take a sheet of blank paper. Think of the term 'research' and jot down what ideas occur to you.
Take a separate sheet of paper and jot down the emotions provoked by the idea of engaging in research.

Comment

For many people, 'research' is something that is either intimidating or boring or perhaps both. It is done by other people, such as psychologists or doctors, using highly complex and technical procedures, rather than social workers. I hope to challenge these myths throughout this book and demonstrate to you that research is something that can be interesting and straightforward.

The aim of this chapter is to provide an accessible and straightforward guide through the challenges you may experience. It has begun by asking you to reflect upon your initial thoughts about engaging in research. In the next part, you will be introduced to key terms and guidance will be offered on planning your project. The stages of the process will be outlined and you will be asked to reflect upon the process of choosing a suitable topic and developing a research question. The distinction between quantitative and qualitative approaches will be discussed and illustrated using case studies of student projects that will be developed further in later chapters. You will be asked to consider a range of research designs from particular traditions to illustrate the wide diversity of approaches.

Key terms in research

As with any new area of study, you need to understand new terminology that can seem technical and confusing. Here are a few key terms that you will come across when studying for your research project. There is considerable debate about the exact use of specific terms, but the definitions below are generally agreed upon and are the meanings used in this book.

Data   refers to the information that you are going to collect in order to answer your research question, for example the words used by your interview participants or numerical information from your questionnaires. Strictly speaking, data is a plural rather than a singular noun (the singular is 'datum') and this convention shall be kept throughout.

Methodology   refers to the totality of how you are going to undertake your research. It includes the research approach that you will use, including your epistemological position and the specific research methods you will choose, e.g. interviews, questionnaires.

Research approach   refers to the traditional division between quantitative and qualitative traditions in research, which will be discussed fully in this chapter.

Research method   refers to the practical ways that you are going to use to collect your data. The four most commonly used methods in student research are interviews, questionnaires, focus groups and documentary analysis. Each method has a separate chapter.

Sampling   refers to the process of selecting the participants (or other data sources, e.g. documents) that will be involved in your study. Your *sample* (the selection of people or other data sources) is chosen from the total possible data sources, known as the *population*.

Research participants   replaces the outmoded term 'research subjects', because the latter term suggests that people involved in research should have a passive role in a process to which they are 'subjected'. The term 'participants' suggests a more active and equal role, in which participation is informed and freely chosen.

Epistemology   is the study of knowledge and addresses the question of what counts as legitimate knowledge. Research projects contain assumptions about what is legitimate knowledge, which is known as its *epistemological position or stance*. This is discussed further in this chapter.

Planning your research

Planning your research properly takes time but it is worthwhile getting it right at the beginning. It is tempting to rush into arranging interviews or focus groups or sending off your questionnaire. Although you may manage in the short term and feel you are 'getting it done', you run the risk of time-consuming problems later because your data do not answer your research question are difficult to analyse.

It is important to allow yourself sufficient time to undertake your research and allow for possible delays. For example, common delays occur when trying to obtain ethical approvals, or participants cancel and you have to rearrange appointments. Similarly, transcribing interviews or focus groups takes longer than most people anticipate and data analysis even more so.

It is worthwhile keeping a research journal or log in which you can jot down ideas, notes of material that you have read, conversations that you have had and to do lists. You can record all of your thoughts as your project develops and include the texts that you identify and the results of your literature searches. It is an invaluable aid to promoting reflexivity, as it enables you to capture and examine your thoughts on the research process, the decisions that you have made and your role as researcher.

A research journal can be invaluable in the early stages to help you clarify your thinking and work through confusions and dilemmas. As you write up your research, it enables you to retrace your steps and remind yourself of earlier stages. Throughout the process, it is very helpful to have all of your material in one place rather than having to sort through separate notebooks or diaries to find a reference or an idea that you jotted down. A popular format is a folder containing A4 sheets that can be taken out and placed into a ring binder as you go along. An alternative is using a bound journal that can be photocopied every 10–15 pages to ensure that the material is not lost.

The six stages of research

Your research project will proceed through six stages, as outlined in Figure 1.1.

Phase	Stage
Phase 1 – Planning	**Stage 1: Choosing your research topic and formulating your research question.** This will be the focus of Chapters 1 and 2.
	Stage 2: Choosing your research approach. This will be the main focus of this chapter and consists of the following stages: • deciding your research approach – qualitative and quantitative research; • deciding your research design, including research method and sampling.
	Stage 3: Undertaking your literature review. This will be discussed in Chapter 2.
Phase 2 – Data collection	**Stage 4: Collecting your data.** See Chapters 3 to 6 for detailed coverage of the main research methods including practical advice.
Phase 3 – Data analysis and writing it up	**Stage 5: Analysing your data.** Making sense of the data that you obtain will be discussed in Chapter 7.
	Stage 6: Writing up your research. The process of presenting your findings and writing up your research will be the focus of Chapter 8.

Figure 1.1 The six stages of research

Choosing your research topic and formulating your research question

The initial stage of the research process is choosing a research topic and developing it into a specific research question. Do not be tempted to formulate complicated questions on the basis that they sound academic. If you read classic research studies, you will find that they have worked well because they have chosen simple, focused research questions.

Your first task is to identify a research topic and formulate your research questions. While the former is often quite easy, the latter can be quite challenging. This is because most students have one or more general areas of interest but translating this into specific research questions usually involves reformulation. We will be discussing this in more depth in Chapter 2, but a brief overview will be provided here.

When choosing your research topic, there are three main considerations:

- *What are you interested in studying?* You may choose a subject to research for a range of reasons, such as personal or professional experience, an interest in the academic subject or an awareness of a gap in the literature. Choose a subject that you are genuinely interested in finding something out about; otherwise it is difficult to maintain enthusiasm over an extended period. Remember that this is likely to be the part of your course where you have the greatest freedom to choose what you study.

- *What will fit your course requirements?* You need to familiarise yourself with the expectations of your institution about the format and scope of your research. Do not underestimate the importance of this, since your overall aim is to complete your social work degree and this will only happen if your research meets the course requirements, however good it may be.

- *What are you able to study?* There are several components to address what it is possible to study. Firstly, what can you ethically research? You need to consider how your research might impact on your participants and other stakeholders. Secondly, what do you have the time and resources to study? An old adage for a research project is: 'Think about what you want to do. Halve it, then halve it again and you may still struggle to get it all done.' Thirdly, what can you get access to study? Many research projects will require you to gain access to participants and you need to consider how practical this is.

It is important that your research question is not so broad that it is unrealistic for you to be able to answer it nor so narrow that it lacks sufficient substance. It is more common for students to have difficulties because their research questions are too broad rather than too narrow.

A traditional recommendation from research supervisors is to be wary of choosing research topics that have attracted considerable recent media attention. The rationale for this is that you are likely to find a considerable amount of media coverage but little research or academic writing. The danger is that the final dissertation will reproduce the generalisations and stereotyping presented in the media reports with little evidence from research studies or academic writing. However, some topics do have a reasonable academic literature and the student may be interested in investigating how the topic has been portrayed in the media. In this case, media coverage would be a legitimate source of data for a documentary analysis (see Chapter 6).

Why formulate an overall research question?

It is important to formulate an overall research question as your project develops because it will focus your choice of research design and your literature search. It is all too easy to find yourself going in several different directions during a literature search or to collect too much unfocused data and then become confused about what to include and what to leave out.

You may find that you have more than one overall research question. If so, they need to link well to form an overall research project. If you find that you have two entirely separate research questions, you probably have two research projects and you need to decide which one you want to undertake.

Choosing your research approach and design – quantitative and qualitative research

Once you have formulated an initial research topic, you need to consider which research approach and research methods to choose. Social research has traditionally been divided into *quantitative* and *qualitative* approaches. These approaches have different views about the nature of knowledge and have different methods and priorities. Although this distinction is contested (Layder, 1993), it is commonly used and there is little evidence of it abating (Bryman, 2008).

Quantitative research tends to emphasise quantification and measurement which can be analysed using statistical tests to establish a relationship between variables, e.g. poor mental health and social exclusion. This can lead to testable hypotheses, which are predictions, e.g. the hypothesis that higher levels of mental ill health are likely to be linked to higher levels of social exclusion.

Qualitative research tends to emphasise words as data, such as the words of participants in interview or written data from documents. Rather than seeking to develop specific testable hypotheses, qualitative research seeks to explain the meaning of social phenomena through exploring the ways in which individuals understand their social worlds. More recently, data in visual forms such as photographs or films have been an increasingly popular subject of study.

In its simplest formulation, quantitative research asks 'what is going on here?' while qualitative research asks 'what is the meaning of what is happening?' For example, a quantitative study may measure the rates for mental ill health and social exclusion for a sample of mental health service users and find that there is a link, i.e. people with higher rates of mental ill health are likely to experience higher rates of social exclusion. A qualitative study would explore the meaning of what is happening, e.g. whether people with mental health problems are experiencing stigma and prejudice, whether participants are isolating themselves as a means of coping with distressing symptoms or some other explanation. Both approaches can provide useful insights into a particular research topic and there is a growing recognition of the strengths of mixed methodologies (Plano Clarke and Cresswell, 2008). Neither approach is 'better' than the other; it is simply a question of deciding which is more appropriate for your research question.

Quantitative research

Quantitative research tends to follow a traditional scientific model which emphasises 'objectivity' by seeking to remove the values and attitudes of the researcher from the study. There is an emphasis on studying causal relationships and formulating fixed rules for the process of inquiry (Humphries, 2008). Sampling issues are particularly important because of the emphasis on being able to create statistical generalisations that are applicable to the wider population.

Quantitative research and positivism

Quantitative research has been influenced by positivism as an approach to knowledge. Every approach to research has underlying assumptions about the nature of knowledge and the social world, which is referred to as an *epistemological position*. Positivism as an epistemological position traces its intellectual heritage back to Auguste Comte and argues that the traditional scientific method applied in the natural sciences is appropriate to the study of society (Giddens, 1993). From a positivist stance, the researcher is seen as an objective observer whose role is to infer laws that explain relationships between observed phenomena (Giddens, 2006).

Gray (2004) identifies three major claims of positivism:

- Reality is viewed as consisting only of what can be experienced through the senses. Consequently, phenomena that cannot directly be sensed, e.g. people's intentions, wishes and fears, are not suitable as a subject for scientific inquiry.

- Inquiry should be based upon scientific observations rather than philosophical speculation, and therefore on empirical inquiry.

- The natural and human sciences are similar as they share common logical and methodological principles. This includes the belief that facts can be distinguished from values.

While positivism has dominated the social sciences for much of the twentieth century, it has fallen from favour since the 1980s as critics have challenged its core beliefs and its appropriateness for researching the complexities of our social world (Payne and Payne, 2004, p171).

The challenges to positivism have led to a more sophisticated version of the traditional scientific approach known as *realism* which is becoming increasingly influential. This is a broad range of approaches variously named as 'scientific realism', 'critical realism', 'subtle realism' and 'transcendental realism', which each have a slightly different emphasis (Robson, 2002). An increasingly popular approach is *critical realism* (Bhaskar, 1978, 1979, 1990), which believes that there is an external reality but sees the concepts that we use to understand it as a provisional way of knowing rather than a direct reflection of reality. This approach also allows for theoretical content that is not amenable to direct observation, which would not be acceptable in positivism (Bryman, 2008).

Some examples of student projects using a quantitative approach

Here are some examples of student research projects using a quantitative approach.

CASE STUDY

Questionnaires

Varsha is a final year student who is interested in her fellow students' experiences of their social work training. She wants to use questionnaires to study her fellow students' attitudes towards their professional training, particularly whether they feel it is preparing them for the realities of working as qualified social workers. She is interested in whether participants' responses differed according to year of study, age, gender and amount of pre-qualifying experience. For example, Varsha has a hypothesis that older students will report higher levels of confidence in their ability to practise and wants to test this out. (See Chapter 5 on questionnaires for a full discussion of this example.)

CASE STUDY

Documentary analysis

Sarah is a student on a mental health placement. She is interested in how the media portrays women with a diagnosis of schizophrenia and has decided to use documentary analysis for her research project within a feminist paradigm. She could use either a quantitative or qualitative approach, but chooses to use a quantitative method called content analysis. This is a data analysis method that uses objective and systematic counting and recording procedures to produce quantitative data about the manifest, i.e. visible, content of communication. Sarah decided to use an electronic database of newspaper articles from a range of national tabloid and broadsheet newspapers to study coverage of mental health over a one-year period. (See Chapter 6 on documentary analysis for a full discussion of this example.)

Qualitative research

Qualitative research   tends to use data in the form of words rather than numerical information. It seeks to explain social phenomena through understanding the ways in which individuals make sense of their social worlds and sees knowledge as historically and culturally situated (Crotty, 1998, p67). In qualitative research, there are no clearly defined rules about sample size, but generally smaller sample sizes are used and studied in more depth and detail (Miles and Huberman, 1994). The primary focus is being able to understand individuals' own accounts of their perceptions, views and feelings and the meanings they attach to social phenomena.

Qualitative research has been influenced by interpretivism as an epistemological position. *Interpretivism* is a broad term to describe a range of approaches that challenge the traditional scientific approach of positivism. Interpretivism argues that the research methods of the natural sciences are inappropriate to study social phenomena because they do not take into account the viewpoints of the social actors involved. For example, identifying the reasons for youth crime requires the researcher to understand the perspectives of the key social actors. The intellectual origins of interpretivism can be traced back to Weber's notion of *Verstehen*, the hermeneutic-phenomenological tradition and symbolic interactionism (Bryman, 2008).

Quantitative research is generally more valued by governmental bodies as it focuses more on the 'what works' agenda and is more easily generalisable, whereas social work research has tended to favour qualitative approaches. The majority of recent government-funded research has been qualitative research but this is at least partly influenced by the lack of capacity within social work to undertake quantitative research. More recently, there has been a trend towards combining these methodologies and these traditional distinctions have become blurred.

Whereas quantitative research seeks to remove the researcher from the study through addressing issues of bias, qualitative research argues that this is neither possible nor necessarily desirable. We bring our background and identity to our research, but from a traditional perspective this is viewed as a source of bias rather than a valuable component to our research (Maxwell, 1996). This is addressed in qualitative research through the concept of reflexivity, which acknowledges that we bring our own thoughts, values and beliefs as well as our ethnicity, race, class, gender, sexual orientation, occupation, family background and schooling to our research (Kirby and McKenna, 1989).

Reflexivity   has been defined as the *practice of researchers being self-aware of their own beliefs, values and attitudes, and their personal effects on the setting they have studied, and self-critical about their research methods and how they have been applied* (Payne and Payne, 2004, p191). Reflexivity can ensure high standards because it involves the researcher constantly reviewing the process of investigation. Huberman and Miles (1998) argue for the researcher documenting the research process, which has been referred to as an 'audit trail' that explains why decisions were made (Lincoln and Guba, 1985). However, this should be regarded as a resource rather than a defensive action (Payne and Payne, 2004). Reflexivity has been particularly stressed in feminist research as part of the rejection of patriarchal forms of research and as a resource for a radical paradigm shift (Payne and Payne, 2004).

Feminist research has a long tradition of promoting qualitative research as an appropriate strategy for studying social phenomena in context. Feminist research is not so much a specific research design or method but an approach to research that is informed by a set of values. These values recognise the power differentials that exist within wider society and within academic discourses which have favoured patriarchal models of research that emphasise objectivity and distance between the researcher and the researched. As such, it tends to be anti-positivist although it includes quanti-tative as well as qualitative research methods. It places gender at the centre of social inquiry, investigating and representing the diversity of women's perspectives (Saran-takos, 2005).

Some examples of student projects using a qualitative approach

---

CASE STUDY

Focus group
Patrick is on placement in a large, local authority family centre. He is interested in social workers' views on the barriers to fathers being involved in parenting assessments.

He decided that a focus group would be a good research method because it would enable him to hear a range of views and for participants to interact with each other and challenge one another's views. Patrick's focus is on participants' professional experi-ence rather than their personal biographies and it would take much longer to conduct interviews that would produce a similar amount of data. The disadvantages of focus groups are that it can be difficult to arrange for a group of people to meet and the possibility that some group members will not feel able to express their opinions.

Patrick considered how to select his participants and how many focus groups to run. Eight staff members were interested in being involved and Patrick contacted a neigh-bouring family centre and managed to recruit eight staff members which would enable him to run two focus groups.

CASE STUDY

Interviews
Victoria is a social work student on placement in a voluntary sector mental health orga-nisation. She is interested in how voluntary sector staff view working in partnership with statutory sector mental health organisations and would like to use qualitative interviews to explore this further.

Victoria must decide who to include in her sample. She considered that the most appro-priate strategy would be purposive sampling, in which she selects participants who are

→

CASE STUDY *continued*

most likely to yield useful information. This is often based upon factors such as the participant's knowledge, experience or role. She decided to interview two groups of voluntary sector staff, one working in her placement agency and another in a similar voluntary organisation in a neighbouring area. She will focus on staff members who are likely to experience partnership working as part of their everyday role.

Do I really have to discuss epistemology?

In the last two sections, we have discussed some of the main epistemological positions that have influenced quantitative and qualitative approaches. A common student question is whether it is necessary to talk about epistemology in your final dissertation. The extent to which you are expected to be explicit about your epistemological position depends upon whether you are completing an undergraduate or postgraduate degree and the requirements of your individual institution. Most postgraduate courses require you to discuss your epistemological position and many undergraduate courses do not, but this varies between institutions.

Either way, the important point is to not be intimidated by the terminology, but to read around the different approaches and make sure the approach you choose is relevant to your data collection methods. Imagine that your epistemological position, design and research methods are like different items of clothing. For example, if you choose a qualitative approach with an interpretative epistemology then choose a highly structured questionnaire, this is similar to choosing clothes that clash with each other. While each item may be acceptable individually, the combination does not work. Making the different items match is an important part of making your project credible.

Research designs from particular traditions

You will now be asked to consider a range of research designs that come from particular traditions. This is not exhaustive and it is not intended as a menu that you must choose from. The aim is to illustrate the rich diversity in approaches to research design and the values that underpin them. The approaches are discussed in alphabetical order to challenge the idea that some designs are 'better' than others. The 'best' research design is the one that answers your research question.

Action research and participatory action research

Action research challenges the traditional conception of the researcher as separate from the real world, seeking theoretical knowledge that makes little difference in practice. It is associated with smaller-scale research projects that seek to address real-world problems, particularly among practitioners who want to improve practice.

Rather than merely studying the social world, action research seeks to change it in practical ways. Another feature of action research is a view of the research process as being cyclical, in the sense that findings are fed back directly into practice in an ongoing process (Denscombe, 2007).

Action research traces its intellectual history to the work of Kurt Lewin, a social psychologist working in poor communities in postwar America (Humphries, 2008). Action research is not a specific research method. It is more an approach to research that stresses the importance of links with real-world problems and a belief that research should serve practical ends. It is compatible with a wide range of research methods, ranging from an experimental to a phenomenological design.

Participatory action research (PAR) is a form of action research that is committed to the involvement of those who are most affected (Alston and Bowles, 1998). It challenges the traditional power imbalance between the researcher as 'expert' and research participant as 'passive subject' and is highly compatible with anti-discriminatory and anti-oppressive practice.

There are also a number of similar approaches, such as 'appreciative inquiry' and 'co-operative inquiry', which share a commitment to promoting the empowerment of participants but each have different emphases (Heron and Reason, 2006; Ludema, et al., 2006).

These are fascinating and increasingly influential forms of research, but their innovative nature makes these methods highly problematic for university courses. Genuine participatory research requires considerable time to develop and careful thought needs to be given to whether it can be achieved within your timescales.

Case Studies

A case study is a detailed inquiry into a single example of a phenomenon, whether it is an organisation, individual, event, process, location or period of time (David, 2006). Rather than a research method, it is more a focus of study in which a variety of research methods can be used. These can range from experimental methods within a quantitative approach through to ethnography using observation and interviews within a qualitative approach. In practice, however, most case studies tend to adopt a qualitative approach (Payne and Payne, 2004).

Yin (2003) argues that case study research has traditionally been regarded as a 'weak sibling' compared to other research designs such as experimental studies. This has changed in recent years, as qualitative research has become more accepted within the social sciences. A traditional criticism of case studies is whether findings can be generalised. For example, the statistical generalisations produced by large-scale quantitative analysis would not be possible, but this would be inappropriate because the case is studied in its own right rather than as an example of a particular class (Payne and Payne, 2004).

Yin (2003) identifies three types of case study. The *critical case* is chosen because it has features that challenge an existing theory or hypothesis. The *unique case* is chosen because its distinctiveness is its merit, although it may provide ways of understanding more usual cases. The *revelatory case* is chosen because it can provide new insights and ideas.

Evaluation research

Evaluation research has become popular within social work as part of the drive for increased accountability of public services and the evidence-based practice agenda. Indeed, it is usually valued highly by practitioners, particularly when deciding between different interventions or resources that are available.

To evaluate something is to assess its merits or worth. By definition, it cannot be value neutral because there must be aims and standards against which something is judged (Humphries, 2008, p170). In real life, evaluation is also rarely value neutral in the sense that it can be used for organisational purposes. For example, evaluations can be used to justify closing a service or to promote the wider organisation.

Evaluation research requires you to develop specific criteria, which can be an interesting and fraught process as different stakeholders can have different perspectives. Senior management may be interested in cost-effectiveness and adherence to national standards, while service users may be more interested in how responsive the service is to their needs. There are obvious similarities with action research. However, one common difference is the role of the researcher. While the researcher in action research is often in a practitioner role, this is less acceptable within evaluation research because it would be viewed as compromising the objectivity of the researcher.

If you are considering evaluating a service or intervention for your research project, you may find that existing data have been collected that you can utilise. However, you need to ensure that your project constitutes research rather than just audit. For example, an evaluation of a day centre for people with learning disabilities may include information about which activity groups are most popular and details of catering arrangements. These are important matters for the day centre to consider in meeting service users' needs and preferences but they probably would not be regarded as research. The key distinction is that your project must seek to generate some generalisable knowledge that is relevant for similar projects elsewhere or for the service user group as a whole.

Another related criticism of evaluation is that it is atheoretical in its approach, i.e. it does not use wider theory drawn from the social sciences to inform its design. In many contexts, this is not problematic but your research study needs to demonstrate that you have engaged with the wider academic literature so you need to give careful consideration to this. A final note of caution is that evaluation research can be politically sensitive, which can pose challenges for access and your relationship with participants.

Having raised these notes of caution, evaluation research is an important and growing area of social work research and deserves serious consideration. Gaining skills in this area can be very useful in your career for enabling you to see beyond what is presented in evaluation reports to the complex and fraught issues that lie underneath.

Experimental and quasi-experimental design

Experimental and quasi-experimental designs are closest to a traditional scientific approach and are most often used to evaluate interventions and test theories. It is sometimes stated that it is the most rigorous form of research, which is somewhat misleading as all forms of research can possess rigour. It is more accurate to state that it is the approach that places most emphasis on removing possible sources of bias, which is achieved through introducing a degree of randomisation at different stages of the process.

The classic experimental design is the randomised controlled trial (RCT), in which participants are randomly assigned to one of two groups: an experimental and a control group. The experimental group receives the intervention while the control group does not, and the effects are then measured in each group. This raises ethical issues, because it requires one group to not receive a beneficial intervention. This is less ethically problematic when there is little evidence as yet that the intervention is effective, but becomes more so as there is increasing evidence that participants would be likely to benefit. This design has been adapted within social work to address these concerns and incorporate social work values. For example, recent randomised control trials of a parenting intervention, Families and Schools Together (FAST), have included a research design that used two different parenting interventions, one person-based and another leaflet-based (McDonald, et al., 2006; Abt Associates, 2001). Another similar study includes a waiting list control group in an 'intervention now' and 'intervention later' design, where every family receives the intervention but one group receives it immediately and another receives it shortly after (Kratochwill, et al., 2004: McDonald, et al., 2006).

Randomised control trials (RCTs) form one end of a spectrum of experimental and quasi-experimental approaches that can be used. A common quasi-experimental design is a pre and post design, in which one group of participants experience an intervention and key variables are measured before and after the intervention to establish whether there has been a change. A recent study by one of the key proponents of experimental approaches, Donald Forrester, combines a pre and post design with an embedded randomised control trial.

RESEARCH SUMMARY

Forrester, et al. (2008) conducted a quasi-experimental evaluation of a two-day training course for 40 child and family social workers in a specific therapeutic model, motivational interviewing (MI), to improve their skills in working with parental alcohol misuse. The

→

study employed a pre and post design, in which data were collected before, during and three months after the training. Data were collected using validated instruments, and qualitative self-reports and, at the three-month follow-up, participants' skills in motivational interviewing were assessed by simulated interviews with clients played by social work students. A randomised control trial (RCT) of the effectiveness of supervision was embedded within the study, in which participants were randomly assigned to an experimental group that received supervision and a control group that did not.

The study found that the two-day training had a modest positive impact on participants' simulated practice, attitudes and qualitative accounts of practice. However, at the three-month stage, skill levels were relatively low and only ten practitioners were able to demonstrate relative competence in motivational interviewing practice. Indeed, the general level of listening skills in child and family social workers was lower than anticipated. There was a low take-up of follow-up supervision and little impact on participants' skill levels. An interesting and thought-provoking finding was that those participants who stated that they already incorporated motivational interviewing into their practice had among the lowest observed skills!

Although experimental and quasi-experimental designs are common within the discipline of psychology, there are surprisingly few examples in the social work field. Key recent studies within social work include RCT studies of a parenting intervention, Families and Schools Together (FAST) developed by Professor Lynn McDonald (Kratochwill, et al., 2004: McDonald, et al., 2006; Abt Associates, 2001) and a range of quasi-experimental studies (Biehal, 2005, 2008). These studies take a traditional scientific design and demonstrate that it can incorporate social work values. There is evidence of a growing momentum of experimental and quasi-experimental approaches within social work with the establishment of a research centre, the Tilda Goldberg Centre at the University of Bedfordshire (www.beds.ac.uk), which promotes the use of these approaches within social work.

Narrative approaches

There has been increasing interest in narrative approaches across the social sciences (Squire, et al., 2008; Gubrium and Holstein, 2009). Narrative approaches are interested in the *storied nature of human conduct* (Sarbin, 1986), in which we respond to experiences by constructing stories and listening to the stories of others.

Narratives have been provisionally defined as *discourses with a clear sequential order that connects events in a meaningful way for a definite audience and thus offers insights about the world* (Hinchman and Hinchman, 1997, pxvi). However, such definitions are in dispute and the process of analysis does not offer the tightly prescribed procedures prevalent in approaches such as grounded theory (Andrews, et al., 2008; Riessman, 1993, 2007).

Elliott identifies the following common themes in narrative research:

- an interest in people's lived experiences and an appreciation of the temporal nature of that experience;

- a desire to empower research participants and allow them to contribute to determining what are the most salient themes in the area of research;

- an interest in process and change over time;

- an interest in the self and representations of the self;

- an awareness that the researcher him or herself is also a narrator.

(Elliott, 2005, p6)

Narrative research is often interested in issues of identity as stories play a central role in the formation of identity (Crossley, 2007, p135). Indeed, Mair asserts that:

Stories are the womb of personhood. Stories make and break us. Stories sustain us in times of trouble and encourage us towards ends that we would not otherwise envision.

(Mair, 1989, p2)

The history of narrative approaches to research can be traced back to two different academic traditions (Rustin, 2000; Andrews, et al., 2004: Squire, et al., 2008). The first is the post-war rise of humanistic approaches within psychology and sociology as a reaction against positivism. The second is the influence within the humanities of a range of developments from Russian structuralist, French poststructuralist, postmodern, psychoanalytic and deconstructionist approaches to narrative (Squire, et al., 2008).

There is a range of approaches to narrative research and a commonly made distinction is between event-centred and experience-centred approaches. Event-centred approaches focus upon *the spoken recounting of particular past events that happened to the narrator* (Squire, et al., 2008, p5) and are influenced by the work of Labov (Labov and Waletsky, 1967). Experience-centred approaches have a broader focus and explore stories that *may be about general or imagined phenomena, things that happened to the narrator or distant matters that they've only heard about* and can include writing and visual materials as well as speech (Squire, et al., 2008, p5).

The interest in people's lived experiences and in questions of identity mean that narrative research is particularly appropriate for understanding the experiences of trauma and researching sensitive issues (Crossley, 2000, 2007). Examples of narrative research include an autobiographical study of cancer (Frank, 1995), a study of men living with a long-term HIV diagnosis (Davies, 1997) and a historical study of how mental health service users' 'voices' have changed over time (Crossley and Crossley, 2001).

Addressing ethical issues and research governance

An important part of planning your research project is addressing ethical issues and following ethical governance processes. Each university has its own system of ethics committees, but there are also similar processes within statutory agencies to protect its service users and staff from unethical research practices.

The NHS research ethics procedure is the most well known, but in 2005 the government introduced the second edition of the Research Governance Framework (Department of Health, 2005) that covers local authorities. Although there have been delays in implementation, this is likely to make a significant difference in social care research. Check out which procedures apply to you at the earliest stages of your research, because you need to consider whether you have sufficient time to address the requirements or whether you need to rethink how to conduct your research.

Although different ethics committees have different practices and priorities, the core issues that ethics committees will be expecting you to address are:

- *Non-malevolence*   Have you taken all reasonable steps to protect your participants from foreseeable harm? For example, interviewing participants can be potentially upsetting and you need to think through how you can ensure they are supported.
- *Informed consent*   You will normally be required to provide written information to potential participants to enable them to make an informed choice.
- *Ethical data management*   How will you anonymise your data and who will have access? How will you store the information that you gain? Have you taken reasonable steps to protect your participants from their data being lost?

A research attitude

Whichever research approach and design you choose, it is important for you to develop a research attitude. This is about being rigorous in your thinking and being willing to challenge yourself and others in a responsible way. This has been expressed by Robson as follows:

- *Being systematic*   Giving serious thought to what you are doing and how and why you are doing it. This involves considering alternatives and making an argument for the choices that you make.
- *Being sceptical*   Subjecting your ideas to scrutiny and possible disconfirmation. This involves asking yourself what evidence you have for the points you are making and considering alternative explanations.
- *Being ethical*   Working within acceptable parameters. This involves following ethical governance processes and thinking about how your research can affect others.

(Robson, 2002, p18)

This will be developed more fully in the next chapter, when we will discuss the key skills involved in adopting a critical and systematic attitude towards research appraisal.

C H A P T E R   S U M M A R Y

The chapter asked you to reflect upon your initial thoughts about engaging in research. You were introduced to key terms in research and the stages of the research process were outlined. You were asked to think about the process of choosing a research topic and developing a research question. The distinction between quantitative and qualitative approaches to research were discussed and illustrated using case studies of student research that will be developed further in later chapters. You were asked to consider a range of research designs from particular traditions to illustrate the wide diversity of approaches. Ethical issues and research governance processes were discussed and key issues were explored.

FURTHER READING

Andrews, M, Squire, C and Tamboukou, M (eds) (2008) *Doing narrative research*. London: Sage.
An excellent introduction to both the theoretical and practical dimensions of narrative research.

Bryman, A (2008) *Social research methods,* 3rd edition. Oxford: Oxford University Press.
An excellent, all-round textbook that covers all aspects of the research process.

Hall, I and Hall, D (2004) *Evaluation and social research: Introducing small-scale practice.* Basingstoke: Palgrave Macmillan.
A useful guide that presents practical advice and real-life examples.

Humphries, B (2008) *Social work research for social justice.* Basingstoke: Palgrave Macmillan.
A good, recent textbook that provides a detailed account of research designs with an evaluation from a social justice perspective.

Kvale, S and Brinkmann, S (2008) *InterViews: Learning the craft of qualitative research interviewing,* 2nd edition. London: Sage.
Second edition of a classic text firmly within the qualitative approach, which provides an interesting and detailed account of the differences between positivist and interpretative approaches.

Macdonald, GM (2001) *Effective interventions for child abuse and neglect: An evidence-based approach to planning and evaluating interventions*. Chichester: Wiley.
A classic text on the evidence-based approach to social work interventions.

Pawson, R and Tilley, N (1997) *Realistic evaluation.* London: Sage.
A classic and provocative text from the realist tradition.

Reason, P and Bradbury, H (eds) (2006) *Handbook of action research.* London: Sage.
A useful collection of chapters by key figures in action research.

Riessman, C (2007) *Narrative methods for the human sciences.* London: Sage.
An updated version of her classic 1993 text.

Yin, R (2003) *Case study research: Design and methods*, 3rd edition. London: Sage.
The classic text on case study design.

Chapter 2

Undertaking a literature review

Introduction

You will have had some thoughts about your research topic and be starting to formulate your research question. The next stage is to undertake a literature review in order to establish what is already known about your research topic. This chapter aims to guide you through that process, using case studies and activities to illustrate the different stages.

It is important to see your literature review as an ongoing process that will start in the early stages of your research and continue throughout the life of your project. This is not just about updating your literature review as new material becomes available. As you undertake your data collection, your data are likely to suggest new ways of looking at your research topic. Consequently, developing your literature review is likely to be a continual process in which you re-engage with the literature as your project develops.

This chapter will begin by defining what is meant by a literature review and exploring its roles and functions. The transition from selecting a research topic to developing a research question will be explored, using the useful tool of concept mapping. The process of undertaking a literature search will be reviewed, focusing on the challenge of finding high-quality material in your topic area.

The procedures for undertaking a literature search and making effective notes will be examined. You will be asked to consider what it means to analyse critically the literature that you find and clear guidelines will be discussed. The process of writing up your literature review will be considered and some of the problems frequently encountered by students will be examined.

What is a literature review?

A literature review is a comprehensive summary and critical appraisal of the literature that is relevant to your research topic. It presents the reader with what is already known in this field and identifies traditional and current controversies as well as weaknesses and gaps in the field.

The terms 'literature search' and 'literature review' are often treated as if they were synonymous. Strictly speaking, a literature search refers to the process of identifying material that is appropriate while a literature review refers to a critical evaluation of that material. In either case, the terms are used to refer to both the process and the resulting document.

In a traditional dissertation format, you will discuss what you found in the body of literature at two stages. Firstly, you will present it in your literature review to demonstrate your understanding of what has already been written in your field. You then revisit it towards the end of your dissertation after you have presented your own findings to discuss any similarities and differences between what you found and what previous researchers have found.

Hart (2001) identifies two key areas when you begin a research project – the literature relevant to your research topic and the literature on research methodology, i.e. how to conduct research. This is an important distinction because you are likely to have only searched for the former during your previous academic study. Reading this book is an excellent start to developing your knowledge of the latter and each chapter contains recommended texts for further reading.

You may have heard about a form of literature review called a *systematic review*. A systematic review is a literature review undertaken using a strict, explicit and transparent set of formal protocols that seek to minimise the chances of systematic bias and error (Macdonald, 2003). Within the field of social work, this is usually commissioned by governmental or national bodies such as Social Care Institute for Excellence

(SCIE) in order to provide guidance about specific areas of practice and does not usually form part of undergraduate research projects.

There are many reasons for undertaking a literature review. It is likely to form a necessary part of your dissertation and may be required instead of an empirical research project (i.e. where you collect your own data). It is an important step in the research process because it enables you to gain an understanding of what has already been written about your topic. This includes reviewing which research designs have been used and the key issues that have been identified. Consequently, it is an essential part of developing expertise in your field, both in the topic area and in research methodology.

Moving from a research topic to a specific research question

For some research projects, the transition from having a research topic to formulating a specific research question is smooth and unproblematic. For others, it can take considerable time to narrow down the research topic and this is usually something that happens in parallel with developing the literature review. When you see how others have approached your research topic and the range of methodologies they have used, this is likely to focus your thinking.

A useful tool technique to aid this process is the concept map, which is a way of visually representing the different elements of your topic. Concept mapping can be a useful way of thinking about your research topic because it helps you to break down your topic into its constituent parts and examine them in more depth.

> **CASE STUDY**
>
> *Susan is a social work student who is interested in how childcare social workers engage fathers when there are child welfare concerns. However, she is unclear how she is going to narrow this topic down to a research question.*
>
> *She has decided to use a concept map to identify the different angles from which she could approach this topic (see Figure 2.1).*

Having completed her initial concept map, Susan decided that she was interested in identifying possible barriers to fathers' involvement.

> **ACTIVITY 2.1**
>
> *Now it is your turn to use a concept map to explore your topic.*
>
> *Write your research area at the centre of a piece of paper and map out the possible topics or angles from which you could approach it. Your aim is to move from a general topic area to a specific research question.*

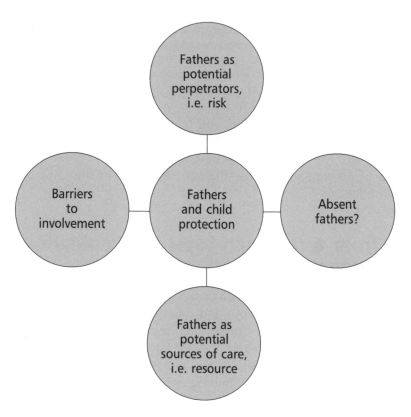

Figure 2.1 Initial concept map

Comment

This can be useful to help you check your current understanding of your research topic. When you first do this, your concept map will represent your initial under-standing of the topic. As you identify literature, you can update your concept map to create a visual representation of what material is available. You may find that there is a concentration of literature on particular topics while other topics receive scant discussion. This will influence your choice and can be a useful subject for discussion in your literature review.

Conducting your literature search

A literature search is the first stage in your literature review and is an organised investigation for material relevant to your topic across a range of sources. In your previous studies, you may have concentrated on using textbooks to inform your coursework. The purpose of textbooks is to provide students with an overview of what is generally agreed in a particular field. Although textbooks may report the results of research studies, they may not be sufficiently current or detailed for the purposes of your literature review. You need to expand the range of literature that you utilise and this should include reading the original research studies themselves to be able to critically appraise them.

There are four main types of literature that will be relevant:

- *Journal articles* in printed and electronic form. These are generally regarded as being of the highest quality because most journals are peer-reviewed. This means that articles submitted to the journals will be anonymised and sent out to reviewers with expertise in the field. These reviewers will evaluate the potential article and will submit detailed feedback that the author must address before it is of a publishable standard. This does not guarantee that everything in an article is correct but it is a relatively stringent. While articles from non-refereed journals may be of a similar standard, they have not been through this process. Journals will state that they are peer-reviewed if this is the case and many search engines allow you to search for refereed journals only.

- *Books* in printed and electronic form. There are good quality control mechanisms built into book publishing, but they are not regarded as being as stringent as for peer-reviewed journals. You may be used to reading textbooks that provide you with a good overview of an area, but the research studies that they describe are likely to be classic studies rather than the most recent material.

- *Official and legal publications* include legislation, policy and discussion documents as well research studies and summaries of research findings in specific subject areas, such as hospital discharge or child protection. As well as governmental bodies, this includes material from other public organisations, e.g. the Joseph Rowntree Foundation, the NSPCC.

- *Grey literature* is material that is not published through traditional, commercial sources but is available through specialised sources, e.g. research reports from local public or voluntary organisations. It is often unclear what quality control systems have been used, but they may contain some very useful and relevant information. Whether you include them in your literature review depends upon what other material you have found. If you have found similar material from more conventional sources, you may not need to include them. But such material can be very valuable, as long as you recognise the relative authority and its strengths and weaknesses.

How do I start my literature search?

The focal point of your literature search will be a systematic examination of a number of bibliographic databases, which will enable you to search effectively across a large number of journals. These are available through your university library, although they are increasingly available to access remotely through your home computer.

Most databases have 'basic' and 'advanced' search engines, so try using the latter for more specific and detailed searches and combine your keywords to find more relevant results. When you search using an electronic database, you will be provided with an abstract that summarises the study. If your university has a subscription to that journal, you will also be able to get access to the full text version. The content of most electronic databases consists of journal articles, but some may include references to other material, such as books, reports and websites. Since no bibliographic database contains every journal published, you will need to search a number of databases to ensure that you identify all of the material available.

It is tempting to immediately start searching, but it is worthwhile putting together a search profile. This will direct your search and consists of the following:

- *Your research question* guides every aspect of your project. For example, 'What are the reasons for delays in hospital discharge for older people?'

- *Keywords* are the main terms that relate to your research question, which you will use as search terms. They should include alternative terms that may be used in the literature, for example using 'older people' but also alternative (and often out-of-date) terms such as 'elderly' or 'geriatric'.

- *Parameters* are any restrictions that will narrow down your search, such as a particular time period or country of research or factors related to the population studied, e.g. age, gender and ethnicity. For example, you decide that you want literature on hospital discharge delay from the UK relating to older people rather than other age groups.

CASE STUDY

Having completed her initial concept map, Susan decided that the research question that she was most interested in was identifying what the barriers were to fathers' involvement in assessments. For her literature search, her first task is to develop a list of keywords that she is going to use.

ACTIVITY 2.2

What will she include in her search profile? What will she include in her research question, keywords and parameters?

Comment

She is already clear about her research question, namely 'What are the barriers to childcare social workers engaging with fathers when there are child welfare concerns?' For her keywords, she felt that 'fathers', 'social work', 'social services' would be relevant to her search. She added 'child protection' and 'family support' because she wanted to have a full range of child welfare concerns. She wanted to include literature from outside the UK but was aware that she would need to restrict it to material in English, as this was her only language. She recognised the need to consider alternative terminology, e.g. 'Department of Human Services' rather than 'Social Services'.

It can be confusing and frustrating at first to use some search engines within libraries because they use Boolean operators. This sounds technical, but it is a relatively simple system to enable you to narrow your search and find the most relevant resources. These are increasingly built into the advanced search functions on electronic databases but it is worth understanding how they work. Although each database uses them in slightly different ways, the general principles apply.

The three most commonly used Boolean operators are 'AND', 'OR' and 'NOT'. If you insert the word 'AND' between search terms, e.g. 'fathers' AND 'child protection', you will narrow your search to texts that contain both terms. If you insert the term 'OR' between search terms, you will broaden your search to include texts that can contain either term. These can usefully be combined, e.g. 'fathers AND child protection OR family support' will identify resources that discuss fathers in the context of either child protection or family support. If you insert the term 'NOT' instead of 'OR', this will exclude any resources containing the second search term. This is useful when it has more than one meaning and you wish to restrict it. For example, if your search term is 'counselling' and you want to exclude careers counselling, you would use 'counselling NOT careers counselling'. Another useful function is the truncation symbol (* ! #), which lets you type in the first part of a word and then the search engine will find alternative endings, e.g. adolesc* will find adolescent, adolescents, adolescence and so on.

It is important to be systematic about your searches to ensure that you have identified all the relevant literature. In Chapter 1, we discussed keeping a research journal in which you record all of your thoughts as your project develops. Having all your material in one place means that you will not have to search through different notebooks or diaries to find a reference. This should include all the searches that you undertake, including the date, bibliographic database and search terms used. A popular method is a folder containing A4 sheets that can be taken out and placed into a ring binder as you go along. An alternative is a handwritten journal, but it is important to photocopy this regularly to ensure that valuable material is not lost if you misplace the journal.

Make a record when you undertake a search, including the keywords you used and the date. You will need to use more than one database because every database has a limited coverage. More importantly, make a reference list as you go along so that you avoid having to search for a reference at the last minute. There are a number of citation software packages such as EndNote, ProCite and RefWorks. Your university is likely to have adopted one and it is worth becoming familiar with it because it will create a central database of references that can be adapted into different citation systems.

An additional search method that can be productive (but far less systematic) is to review the references sections of material that you have already obtained. This can be particularly helpful when you have found an article that directly responds to your research question because the references section is likely to include relevant material. As you gather more articles and books, you may find the same texts being referred to. This usually indicates that these are central texts for your topic and should be included in your literature review. This form of searching can be quite fruitful, but rather haphazard and biased because the writer may not be familiar with all of the literature and may not have included material that they want to distance themselves from. Hence, it should be regarded as a supplement rather than a replacement for a full literature search using electronic databases.

Academic versions of mainstream search engines, such as Google Scholar, are growing in popularity and sophistication. However, it is relatively early days and these are also best regarded as a good supplement rather than a replacement for a full bibliographic search.

Effective reading and note taking

Having identified suitable material, it is important that you are able to use effective reading and note-taking skills to make the most of the time that you have. Rather than printing everything and working your way through a large pile of material, use active reading skills to identify which material is the most relevant and take appropriate notes.

A classic technique (Robinson, 1970) for achieving this is known as the SQ3R reading strategy. It comprises five stages.

1. *Survey (or skim)* Conduct a preliminary scan of the material to get a general sense of what the material is about. This may simply consist of reading the abstract if it is a journal article. Does it look relevant? If not, discard at this stage.

2. *Question* Actively ask yourself what the article or chapter is about and what questions it might answer in order to decide whether the text is worth reading more carefully.

3. *Read* the text more carefully if it has passed the above tests. Read actively, questioning the author's arguments and make appropriate notes.

4. *Recall (or recite)* the main points when you have finished reading, using your own words.

5. *Review* Test yourself to see what you can recall. If there are sections that you cannot remember, you may need to reread the material.

One of the most useful tips for saving time and reducing stress is to make sure that you keep a note of the full reference for the material that you are reading. While this may seem like a nuisance at the time, it is preferable to hunting around for it at the last minute, long after you originally read it.

When you are reading and taking notes, try to make links with other material that you have read. When you read your first article, it is difficult to have a framework to judge it against. When you have read a number of articles, you will have a greater understanding of the literature and will find it easier to evaluate a particular article or book.

> **CASE STUDY**
>
> *Susan developed a system for recording her literature searches and the material that she found. Using her research journal (see Chapter 1), she recorded every search.*
>
> *She read the abstract of every article in order to gain a sense of what it contained. She decided to use a traffic light system to organise the material into three groups (red, amber and green lights). For some articles, reading the abstract was enough for her to realise that the article was not relevant to her research and it was discarded at that stage (red light). Other articles looked very promising and highly relevant to her research topic so were grouped together (green light). A third group were articles that were potentially relevant, depending upon how her research developed (amber light). She decided to devote most of her attention to the 'green light' group in order to develop a good knowledge of her specific research topic but to keep material from the 'amber light' group in case her research changed as it developed.*

What If I find too much or too little material?

As you start your literature search, you may find yourself confronted with either too much or too little material. It is more common to find that your literature search has identified too much material. The development of digital technology has seen a revolution in the information that is available for your research compared to ten or fifteen years ago. The disadvantage of this is that it is easy to become overwhelmed by the sheer volume of information that is available. If you have identified too much material, your search is too broad and needs to be narrowed down. This can be done in a number of ways. Firstly, you could be more specific about your topic. Secondly, you could be more specific about your parameters, e.g. choosing a specific time period or restricting your search to UK materials.

If you have identified too little material, you need to think about your search terms. While some areas really do have very little written about them, it is more likely that your search terms are not fine-tuned enough to pick them up. If you have identified a small amount of material, read it to find out the terminology that is used in your research field. Think of alternative terms and enlist the help of your supervisor and/or fellow students in this task. If you still cannot identify any literature in your research field, it may be necessary to consider adjusting your research topic to ensure you have sufficient material to discuss in your literature review.

Critically analysing the literature

In order to be worth including in your literature search, a text needs to be both relevant and of sufficient quality. Avoid the pitfall of reading material that is interesting but not directly relevant to your research. This can take up a considerable amount of your time and the material is unlikely to feature in your final dissertation.

When you are evaluating a research study, there are a number of questions that you should ask yourself:

- *Research design*   Does the study provide a clear rationale for the choice of research design? Research questions can usually be approached using a variety of research designs so a good study will provide a clear and robust rationale for its choices, including a discussion of why it did not use alternative designs.

- *Data collection methods*   Does the study provide a clear rationale for the choice of data collection methods? For example, a study may have chosen interviews rather than questionnaires or focus groups. Is a coherent account given for this choice? Were known weaknesses addressed and did the data collection methods work in practice?

- *Sampling*   How well do the sampling procedures match the research question? Sampling is particularly important in quantitative research because this limits the extent to which the findings can be generalised. Were known weaknesses addressed and did the sampling procedures work in practice?

- *Data analysis*   How robust is the data analysis? A good study will give a clear account of how the data was analysed, whether it is quantitative or qualitative. Does the data analysis follow the model described? If it is a quantitative study using statistical analysis, are the tests used appropriate? See the end of the chapter for recommended texts on quantitative data analysis and www.social research methods.net provides a useful guide to appropriate statistical tests. If it is a qualitative study, does the analysis provide sufficient context for the material to be understandable? Does it account for the diversity of participants' views?

- *Credibility of the findings*   How credible are the findings? You need to consider whether the conclusions are supported by sufficient evidence and whether they have a consistent logic. It is important to be rigorous about this because we tend to view findings that we agree with as more credible.

- *Generalisability of the findings*   To what extent can the findings be generalised to other settings? For quantitative studies, statistical generalisation is important and this is linked to sampling procedures. For qualitative research, generalisation is not viewed in the same way and the important issue is whether the concepts that are generated are meaningful in other settings. Is the study clear about the extent to which its findings can be generalised to other settings? If so, does this seem reasonable given the limitations of the study?

- *Research ethics*   How does the study address ethical issues? This should include the ethical procedures followed and address issues such as informed consent, ethical data management and how potential risks were avoided. It can also include discussion of the values that underpin the study.

Not all of the literature you identify will be research studies. They may be opinion pieces in which the author puts forward a particular argument or viewpoint based upon their experience or on previous literature. However, many of the same criteria are relevant. Is the argument plausible? What evidence does the author provide to substantiate their claims? Sometimes you may find an article that provides a literature review of your topic area. This may be useful for understanding the key issues and authors. However, do not assume that the author is coming from an impartial perspective. They may have an allegiance to a particular point of view or position and, consequently, they may place less emphasis or even ignore literature that does not support their stance.

Writing up your literature review

Your literature review should provide a coherent and critical account of the literature, identifying patterns and themes as well as evaluating the quality of the material. You need to provide an overall argument or a series of arguments based upon your reading of the literature. Consequently, your literature review should not read like a list of articles and books randomly assembled because this will not demonstrate that you have been able to understand and evaluate the material. As well as evaluating the quality of studies, your analysis should make links between studies, highlighting similarities and differences, for example:

> A number of studies have identified difficulties in engaging fathers
> (Scourfield, 2006; Ghate, 2000). However, the findings have highlighted
> different reasons. Scourfield (2006) identified . . . This can be contrasted with
> Ghate (2000) who found that. . .

You need to have a clear overall structure to your literature review and there are a number of different options. One way is a chronological structure, looking at how your research topic has been written about over a period of time. This is particularly useful when your research topic shows a clear historical development. For example, a literature review of user involvement in mental health could discuss how this has developed using a specific time period. Another alternative is to structure your literature review thematically, focusing on what topics are addressed. Using the same example, the literature review could be structured according to the different philosophies that underpin service user involvement (managerialist *vs* emancipatory models) or the sites of involvement (staff recruitment, service planning and training).

A good literature review will not take what has previously been written at face value but will be aware of the contested nature of knowledge in which alternative views and positions may be taken. It will also be sensitive to issues of power, where some viewpoints are privileged while others are subjugated.

Some common challenges when writing a literature review

There are a number of challenges that students can experience while completing their literature reviews:

- *How do I decide what to include and what to leave out?*   One of the most common problems with literature reviews is that students try to use every piece of material that they have read. This is at least partly because considerable work has gone into identifying and reading the material and the student wants the marker to know this. Although it can be disheartening to leave out material that you have worked hard on, it is almost essential to do this if you want to write a good literature review. The marker will want you to demonstrate that you are developing the ability to construct an argument, which requires you to include only material that is directly relevant to the points that you are making.

- *How far should I go back?*   How far you go back depends entirely upon your research focus, e.g. including classic studies could be highly relevant for some research projects. You can include a time limit on how far you go back, but you need to provide a justification for this. Whichever approach you take, you are expected to have a good grasp of current developments. If you have no material from the last ten years, it may appear that you have not developed your literature searching skills sufficiently. It is possible that there really is no literature from the last decade, but you need to explain this and what measures you have taken to find it.

- *What if I search for literature relating to my topic and there is not a great deal out there? How do I write about this in my dissertation?*   It is always helpful to be explicit in your dissertation about how you conducted your literature search, for example, 'I used the Applied Social Sciences Index Abstracts (ASSIA) and Social Care Online databases using the following search terms,'... This is particularly important if the literature that you identify is rather limited, because it helps convince the reader that you have made a concerted and systematic attempt to identify relevant material. If your literature is extremely sparse, you need to consider whether you've chosen a suitable topic for your project, because it can be difficult to write your literature review and for you to discuss the significance of your findings without responding to a body of literature.

C H A P T E R   S U M M A R Y

This chapter began by defining what is meant by a literature review and exploring its roles and functions. The transition from selecting a research topic to developing a research question was explored, using the tool of concept mapping. The process of undertaking a literature search was reviewed, focusing on the challenge of finding high-quality material in your topic area.

The procedures for undertaking a literature search and making effective notes were examined. You were asked to consider what it means to critically analyse the literature that you find and clear guidelines have been discussed. The process of writing up your literature review was considered and problems frequently encountered by students were examined.

Fink, A (2005) *Conducting research literature reviews: From the internet to paper*, 2nd edition. London: Sage.
A useful guide which focuses on evaluating quantitative research and provides an outline of appropriate statistical tests when appraising research evidence.

Greenhalgh, T (2000) *How to read a paper,* 2nd edition. London: BMJ Publishing.
A book-length guide to appraising research papers from both quantitative and qualitative traditions.

Greenhalgh, T and Taylor, R (1997) How to read a paper: Papers that go beyond numbers (qualitative research). *British Medical Journal*, 315: 740–3.
A classic article that provides a clear account of evaluating qualitative research studies.

Hart C (1998) *Doing a literature review: Releasing the social science research imagination*. London: Sage.
A classic text on compiling your literature review that gives detailed guidance on structure and evaluating arguments.

Newman, T, Moseley, A, Tierney, S and Ellis, A (2005) *Evidence-based social work: A guide for the perplexed*. Lyme Regis: Russell House.
A useful and interesting guide to understanding evidence-based practice within social work. It includes a particularly useful chapter on understanding statistics.

Social Care Institute for Excellence (SCIE) (**www.scie.org.uk**) has a dedicated student section and Social Care Online (**www.scie-socialcareonline.org.uk**) provides an extensive database of information and resources related to social care.

Intute Virtual Training Suite (**www.vts.intute.ac.uk/**) is based at Bristol University and provides online training to enable you to make the most effective use of online resources. They cover all subjects and the specialist portal for social work can be found at **www.vts.intute.ac.uk/he/ tutorial/social-worker**.

The Web Center for Social Research Methods is a US-based resource that provides useful material, including content on choosing appropriate statistical tests and concept mapping (**www.socialresearchmethods.net**).

Joseph Rowntree Foundation (**www.jrf.org.uk**). The Joseph Rowntree Foundation is a national research and development charity that funds a range of research into social policy and publishes its findings on its website.

Chapter 3
Interviews

Introduction

This is the first of four chapters that will introduce you to commonly used research methods and will provide an overview of how interviews can be used effectively for research purposes. Interviews are one of the most popular research methods for social work students and feel intuitively 'familiar' because of their use in everyday social work practice. They are popular in the social sciences generally and are used in the majority of published qualitative research articles (Silverman, 2005, pp238–9).

This interest in interviews is not confined to social work research. Scourfield (2001) argues that we live in an 'interview culture', in which we are constantly exposed to the idea that something valuable can be learnt by talking one-to-one with another person. Interviews are intuitively 'human', a face-to-face interaction that enables you to communicate with your participants in depth and offers the opportunity to follow up interesting responses. Interviews can enable people to tell their story and are particularly attractive when researchers want to explore people or communities that have traditionally been ignored, misrepresented or suppressed in the past.

In this chapter, you will be asked to consider the advantages and disadvantages of interviews and when it would be most appropriate to use them. Practical issues raised by using interviews will be emphasised through a case study and student-centred activities.

When should interviews be used?

Interviews are best used for research that focuses on the knowledge, values, beliefs and attitudes of participants. They are particularly good at helping participants to think through, consider and make explicit things that have previously been implicit. Robson (2002) argues that facts and behaviour are more easily obtained than beliefs and attitudes, though participants may experience memory lapses or bias, so specific questions about things in the present or recent past are best. Questions about a participant's beliefs and attitudes are more complex because responses may be affected by the wording and sequence of questions, but the use of multiple questions and scales can help.

Interviews or questionnaires?

A common dilemma for students is deciding whether to use interviews or question-naires. The advantages that interviews have over questionnaires are that interviews are good at examining complex issues and producing rich data and they enable participants to discuss sensitive issues in an open way without committing themselves in writing. The disadvantages are that interviews are more time-consuming to com-plete than questionnaires and it is more complex and time-consuming to analyse interview data.

Interviews or focus groups?

Another dilemma is whether to use interviews or focus groups. While focus groups are effective in accessing shared, public knowledge, interviews are fruitful for more per-sonal, biographical information. Interviews can be used in conjunction with focus groups where participants may disclose more sensitive information than they would in a group setting. See Chapter 4 on focus groups for a more detailed discussion.

Types of interview

Although there is a range of different types of interview, the three main forms are structured, unstructured and semi-structured interviews.

Structured or standardised interviews

These are highly ordered and tightly designed interviews designed to collect data that can be quantified. You may have experienced a market research interview, in which multiple-choice questions with a fixed number of responses are used, but they can also be used in the social sciences. Structured interviews have the strength that they are able to produce quantitative data in a clear, readily analysable form. However, they are less popular with students because the closed nature of questioning does not give them sufficient scope to address more complex, rich, qualitative issues.

Structured interviews are part of the quantitative survey research tradition and are similar to questionnaires, which will be discussed in Chapter 5. The remaining forms of interview are generally regarded as part of the qualitative research tradition and form the focus of this chapter.

Unstructured interviews

At the opposite end of the spectrum, unstructured interviews are very open and range from a single question to a list of topics to cover. Sometimes students consider unstructured interviews because they 'want the data to speak for itself'. Others consider it because they lack confidence in constructing a good interview schedule or are unsure about exactly what they want to focus on. The difficulty is that they then produce a number of interview transcripts that are very individual and often do not cover the same ground. This can be a strength for the more experienced researcher who is confident in their abilities to analyse diverse and complex data but a real challenge to the novice researcher. Consequently unstructured interviews are best left to the more experienced researcher.

Semi-structured interviews

This is the classic structure for qualitative research in the social sciences and the most commonly used format in student research projects. In semi-structured interviews, the researcher develops a list of questions known as an *interview schedule*. However, there is some flexibility during the interview, e.g. if a participant introduces a topic earlier than anticipated, the researcher can change the order of questions. The format is popular because it enables you to have sufficient structure to facilitate data analysis while giving you sufficient flexibility to explore participants' responses in depth.

Recruiting and selecting participants

One of the most commonly asked questions is *how many people should I interview?* To some extent, this will be determined by the requirements of your course and may be set by your university. Consequently, discussing this with your supervisor or tutor is the best first step.

This chapter will focus on sampling strategies for using semi-structured or unstructured interviews within a qualitative approach, which is by far the most common approach used in student research projects. If you are planning to employ structured interviews using large sample sizes in a similar way to questionnaires, appropriate sampling strategies will be discussed in depth in Chapter 5. For a general introduction to sampling in both quantitative and qualitative research, see Chapter 1.

In qualitative interviewing, the most common approach is non-probability sampling and the specific sampling strategies used are as follows:

- *Convenience sampling* (sometimes known as accidental sampling) simply means selecting participants based upon the relative ease with which they can be contacted. With convenience sampling, researchers are not interested in how representative any participant is or whether the participant has particular knowledge or experience. Rather, they are looking for participants that are relatively easy to contact. While this is the least credible of sampling techniques, Bryman (2008) argues that this is far more prevalent than is often recognised in social science research.

- *Purposive sampling* (otherwise known as judgemental sampling) is a procedure in which the researcher chooses participants who, in their judgement, are likely to yield useful information. This is often based upon factors such as the participant's knowledge, experience or role. Interviews are most successful when participants have significant experience in the research topic and are likely to want to discuss it. This is the most commonly used sampling method in student research projects and most writers on qualitative research based on interviews recommend it as the procedure of choice (Bryman, 2008, p333).

- *Theoretical sampling* is an approach, developed as part of grounded theory (Glaser and Strauss, 1967: Strauss and Corbin, 1998), which does not predetermine the number of participants that will be interviewed at the beginning of the study. Instead, researchers will carry on interviewing participants until 'saturation' has been achieved, where no significantly new data is being produced and the themes have been exhausted (Strauss and Corbin, 1998). It has been argued that purposive sampling and theoretical sampling are effectively synonymous (Brink 1991; Lincoln and Guba, 1985).

- *Snowball sampling* is a technique where the researcher selects a small number of participants and asks them to recommend other suitable people who may be willing to participate in the study. This is suitable when participants are difficult to identify and contact, such as sex workers or people who are homeless.

- *Quota sampling* is a procedure in which the researcher decides to research groups or quotas of people from specific subsections of the total population. Common categories are demographic such age, gender and ethnicity, but could be related to the research topic. This is rarely used in academic research, but is frequently used in market research (Bryman, 2008).

Victoria is a social work student on placement in a voluntary sector mental health organisation. She is interested in how voluntary sector staff view working in partnership with
statutory sector mental health organisations and would like to use qualitative interviews
to explore this further.

ACTIVITY **3.1**

Victoria must decide who to include in her sample. Which approach might she choose?

Comment

Victoria does not need to use convenience or snowball sampling because she has a
number of potential participants that she can contact relatively easily. Since she is not
using grounded theory to analyse her data, theoretical sampling is not necessary and
quota sampling is rarely used in academic research. The most appropriate sampling
strategy would be purposive sampling, in which she selects participants who are most
likely to yield useful information. This is often based upon factors such as the participant's knowledge, experience or role. She decided to interview two groups of
voluntary sector staff, one working in her placement agency and another in a similar
voluntary organisation in a neighbouring area. She will focus on staff members who
are likely to experience partnership working as part of their everyday role.

Ensuring that your data can be analysed

One of your main aims is to ensure that your data is readily analysable (Arksey and
Knight, 1999). This cannot be overemphasised, because it is relatively easy to spend
time and effort collecting significant amounts of interview data that you later discover
are extremely difficult to analyse.

How easy it is to analyse your data depends mainly upon two factors. The first is how
structured your interview will be, since the more structured the interview, the easier it
will be to analyse the data you produce (Kvale, 1996). However, a certain amount of
flexibility may be appropriate for your research topic. The second issue is how diverse
your participants are in terms of experience, role or other factors. One of the most
common pitfalls is to choose a sample of participants with such a wide range of roles
or backgrounds that the interview data is difficult to analyse.

ACTIVITY **3.2**

Imagine that you are a student who is interested in exploring the impact on older people
of moving into residential care. You are deciding who to interview and are considering
interviewing a service user, a relative, a care manager, a care assistant and a residential
home manager. What problems may this raise for data analysis?

Comment

Although you would gain an enormous breadth of views, it would be very difficult to develop an interview schedule and to analyse the interview data. This is because all of the participants have very different roles so it would be quite challenging to devise questions that would be relevant to all participants. It would be equally challenging to analyse participants' answers because there may be few similarities between the accounts. It could be similar to trying to write an essay in which you compare the colour red, the number seven and the country Belgium (Thurlow Brown, 1988). It also raises ethical issues because it is very difficult to anonymise participants' comments if you have chosen people from different agencies. For example, if you interview one person from a particular agency, you may present your findings as 'The participant from the voluntary agency stated that...' Since there is only one participant from a voluntary agency, it is often easy for readers who are familiar with the agencies to be able to identify the staff member who is being referred to. It is more realistic to choose a smaller number of perspectives, such as service users and carers or care managers and residential staff, in order to ensure that your data can be analysed and reported in a straightforward way.

Developing an interview schedule

Your interview schedule is a written plan of how you are going to structure the interview, including what questions you are going to ask and approximately in what order. When developing your interview schedule, your aim is to ensure that your overall research question is answered while promoting a natural flow of conversation that encourages your participants to talk in an open and relaxed way.

Do not be tempted to go into interviews with a few vague ideas and hope that you can muddle through. The data you get will be muddled and it will take much longer to analyse that data later. Time spent developing a good interview schedule will save you considerable time and stress in the longer term.

During the initial stage of developing an interview schedule, it can be helpful to meet up with a few interested people to generate possible interview questions. Ideally, this would include at least one person who would fit the criteria for your sample because they may spot problems that others may miss. Likely people to invite could include your practice assessor, placement colleagues and fellow students as well as any party that is interested in your specific research topic.

Once you have generated a range of possible questions in the group, take these away to work on them on your own. Review them and discard any that are clearly not relevant. Then divide them into two groups, 'need to know' and 'nice to know' (Krueger and Casey, 2000). 'Need to know' questions are vital to answering your research question, while 'nice to know' questions are ones that you are simply curious about. Material that you gather from 'nice to know' questions will probably never be analysed and make it into your research project. Be honest and ruthless about this and you will probably be surprised by how many fall into the latter category. It may be helpful to arrange another time to meet up with the group when you can test out the questions that you have selected and discuss the order in which they should be asked.

When you have finished the first draft of your interview schedule, identify someone who would fit your sample and interview them as a pilot. This can make significant improvements to your interview schedule because you will realise that some questions do not work for several reasons. Firstly, they may be unclear and participants need to ask clarifying questions. Secondly, they may seem like interesting questions but they do not lead to interesting data that is helpful for your project. Thirdly, you are asking about a subject about which participants have insufficient knowledge so you spend valuable interview time responding to their requests for more information. If your pilot is reasonably successful, you may be able to use the data that you collected.

CASE STUDY

Victoria has decided to use semi-structured interviews and the next stage is designing an interview schedule. She arranged a meeting with her practice assessor and another staff member to generate some ideas for questions. Using a flipchart and pen, they generated as many questions as possible.

Victoria then took these away and worked on her own to decide which questions were most relevant to her overall research question. She wanted to ensure that she used a full range of questions in her interviews.

Types of interview question

From earlier stages in your social work degree, you will already be aware of different types of question that can be useful for interviews. Although transferable, you may find that the approach for research purposes is slightly different. For example, you will be familiar with open and closed questions. An open question allows participants to respond to the question in whatever way they wish. A closed question presents participants with a fixed range of responses that they must select from. You will be familiar with this distinction from other parts of your course and it is likely that you will have been encouraged to use open rather than closed questions in work with clients. In research, both are acceptable and the extent to which you use either form depends largely upon how structured your interview is going to be.

A structured interview will usually have predominantly closed questions, while an unstructured interview will predominantly use open questions. A semi-structured interview will usually have mostly open questions, though having a number of closed questions can be appropriate.

It is important to be aware of the full range of interview questions that are available to you. Kvale (1996, pp 133–5) identifies the following types of interview questions:

- *Introductory questions*   open up the discussion and encourage participants to respond to the research topic in an open way, for example: *Can you describe an experience of...?* These opening questions can lead to rich, descriptive accounts that can be followed up as the interview proceeds.

- *Follow-up questions* encourage the participant to expand on their answers. This can be through questioning or responses that encourage further elaboration. For example, a counselling technique called endpoint highlighting can be employed, which consists of repeating back the last part of the participant's previous sentence. This can be effective, but should be used sparingly. Skills that you are developing in active listening and communicating with service users are central, for example picking up on words or phrases that the participant uses that have particular significance for them.

- *Probing questions* enable you to identify particular responses that you would like further information on without directing the participant's responses, for example *Can you say more about that? Have you had any similar experiences?*

- *Specifying questions* enable you to obtain more precise accounts of what the participant has described. This is particularly helpful if participants are giving rather general, abstract responses, for example: *How important is that compared to other factors? If you had to rate both factors, which would be more important?*

- *Direct questions* allow you to introduce topics, for example: *Have you had any negative experiences of working in partnership with other agencies?* These are best used later in the interview when the participant has had an opportunity to indicate which aspects of the topic are most important to them.

- *Indirect questions*, for example: *How comfortable do you think your fellow students would be in working with a service user with a number of violent offences?* These can enable you to obtain the participant's views about other parties but they are particularly useful for sensitive topics that participants may have difficulty answering directly. Careful follow-up questioning would be necessary to establish whether the participant's response was giving a straightforward account of their beliefs about fellow students or whether they were giving an indirect account of their own feelings.

- *Structuring questions or statements* organise the overall form and order of the interview. They are particularly useful when the participant has either exhausted a topic or moved on to a topic unrelated to the research, for example: *I would like us to look at a new topic . . . Can we get back to when you were talking about . . .*

- *Silence* can be very effective in giving your participant time to think through their responses and add further information that they may have omitted in a more structured and fast-paced interview. Occasionally researchers may experience what therapists call 'door knobbing', where a client discloses vital information as they are leaving the room, literally with their hand on the doorknob. Indeed, Bryman (2008) recommends leaving the tape recorder running as long as possible rather than switching it off immediately for this reason. Allowing a reasonable amount of silence can help provide space during the interview and can indicate that the researcher is genuinely interested in what the participant has to say. However, leaving too long a silence can be uncomfortable for the participant and disturb the flow so careful judgement is required.

- *Interpreting questions* can consist of rephrasing a respondent's statement to check your understanding or clarify what they meant. It can also mean encouraging the participant to explore new links that may be implicit in what they are saying, for example: *Can you see any connection between how you think that social workers are viewed and your attitude towards interprofessional working?*

Using vignette questions

An interesting and useful form of questioning is the vignette, which is a simulation of real events depicting hypothetical situations (Wilks, 2004, p80). The most usual way of presenting information is through written material, but alternative formats such as video material and even cartoons have been used (Wilks, 2004). Vignettes present a scenario to participants who are then asked about their attitudes, beliefs and responses. For example, in the case study Victoria could present a scenario in which there was a dilemma about interagency working. She could then ask participants how they would react in the scenario and explore the reasoning behind their choices.

The advantage that vignette questions have over more general questions is that they root the question in a specific situation. For example, if general questions were used to ask practitioners how they assess risk when they receive a referral, each may respond with broad comments that would be difficult to compare. If the same practitioners were presented with a specific scenario, they are all responding to the same information so it would be easier to compare their responses. They can be particularly effective when dealing with sensitive issues, since vignettes present a hypothetical scenario that can make it less confrontational than asking participants about their own experiences (Finch, 1987).

Vignettes can have more than one stage. For example, a scenario is presented and participants are asked for their immediate responses. They are then presented with further information as the vignette develops and asked about their responses given the new information, which can be used to explore the effect of specific factors.

What questions should I avoid?

There are general rules about what to avoid when developing your interview questions. Try to avoid questions that encourage your participants to engage in abstract generalisations, for example: *What do the media think about young people who commit crimes?* Participants provide better quality data when they are asked about issues rooted in their own concrete experience.

Avoid double-barrelled questions, for example: *Do you support user involvement in recruiting staff and in training courses?* Participants may have different responses to the different parts of the question and are likely to respond to only one part. Similarly, if questions are too long, participants are likely to remember only part of the question.

Be careful of leading questions, that is questions that suggest a particular response. While it can be relatively easy to spot questions with this form of bias, it is all too easy to show non-verbal approval or disapproval of views that you agree or disagree with without realising it.

It is important to make sure that your questions are not repetitive. It is quite common for interview schedules to ask the same question in different forms, which is confusing to participants. If you ask participants questions that require memory recall, ensure that the expectations are realistic, for example, do not ask: *Have you completed more assessments this year compared to five and ten years ago?*

Ensure that your questions are clear to avoid confusion and wasting valuable interview time explaining what you mean. Questions involving jargon are likely to antagonise participants and require you to engage in lengthy explanations, for example: *How are Articles 8 and 12 of the Human Rights Act having an impact on social work?'* Try your questions out on colleagues, fellow students or friends to test whether they are clear.

Be very careful about phrasing questions that can sound confrontational. While challenging questions can produce interesting responses, confrontational questions can cause offence and participants may become guarded or even refuse to continue with the interview. The difference between a challenging question and a confrontational question is often careful wording. Place these towards the end of the interview because you will have had an opportunity to build up rapport and, if the interview is terminated, you will lose less data.

There are mixed views about asking 'why' questions. While the responses can be interesting, participants can experienced it as a cross examination. 'Why' questions suggest to participants that they should provide a rational response to what might be a decision based upon impulse, habit, tradition or other non-rational process (Krueger and Casey, 2000). If so, participants are likely to provide an intellectual rationalisation that bears little relation to the real process.

And finally, ensure that your interview questions link directly with your research question. It can be tempting to imagine yourself with the participant and to design questions that relate to promoting a relaxed, interesting conversation but which do not answer your research question directly. If you design a good interview schedule, when participants have answered all of your interview questions, the data should have answered your research question(s) and no more.

CASE STUDY

Having met with her practice assessor and another staff member to generate some ideas for questions, Victoria took these away to redraft them and then grouped them together to ensure that they were in the right sequence. She realised that some questions were very similar and others were interesting but not directly relevant to her overall research question. Having decided which questions to use, she grouped the questions together and decided the order in which she would ask them. The final version of her interview schedule is shown below in Figure 3.1.

Research question – What are the views of mental health voluntary sector staff about partnership with statutory sector mental health organisations?	
Background	**Interview questions**
Introduction This is to remind participants of who you are and the nature of your research and to address ethical issues.	Introduce myself and remind them about my role as a social work student undertaking a research project as part of my course. Thank the participant for agreeing to be interviewed. Remind them of the information sheet that they have already received, including arrangements around confidentiality. Give brief description of research. Check participant is okay with recording interview. Discuss consent form – participant to sign. Remind participants that they can withdraw at any point.
Personal details form Gaining background information about participant.	Ask participant to complete the personal details form, which asks their name, contact details, experience and qualifications. Explain to participant that their personal details will be stored separately from their interview transcript.
Introductory phase Research question: How do staff members describe partnership working in relation to individual service users and service development?	*How would you describe your experiences of working in partnership with statutory mental health services?* Prompt questions – *Has the partnership working been linked to individual service users? In relationship to service development and planning? Can you describe a fairly typical example of this (without naming individual service users)?* Rationale: This is an introductory question that starts the discussion and encourages participants to respond to the research topic in an open and candid way.
Main body of interview Overall research question: How do voluntary sector workers perceive statutory sector staff? How do voluntary sector workers believe they are perceived?	*If you had to use three words to describe statutory sector workers, what three words would you choose?* (Prompt question – Could you say more about why you chose those particular words?) *If I were to ask them for three words to describe voluntary sector workers, what words do you think they would use.* (Prompt – Could you say more about why you chose those particular words?) Rationale: Indirect questions allow you to explore the participant's beliefs about how they are perceived by statutory sector staff. More creative questions can enable you to get beyond factual accounts to capture more subtle aspects.
Overall research question: How do staff members evaluate partnership working relating to individual service users?	*What do you think are the most positive and least positive aspects of working with statutory agencies?* Rationale: Direct questions are useful to encourage participants to evaluate their experiences.
Concluding questions	*Overall, how would you rate partnership working on a scale of 1 to 10, where 1 is very poor and 10 is very good?* *Could you say more about why you'd give it that rating?* *And finally, what do you think would help improve partnership working?* (Ignore if rated 10 out of 10!) Rationale: These are specifying questions that ask participants to provide precise, detailed, explicit, definite, unambiguous information. Using a scale to rate partnership provides simple numerical data that is easy to analyse combined with qualitative data to explain the meaning.
Closure Enables participants to prioritise the issues discussed and provides an opportunity to discuss any issues not already addressed.	Is there anything that you want to discuss that hasn't come up? Have I covered everything? Thank participant for contributing.

Figure 3.1 Interview schedule

Advantages and disadvantages of interviews

Interviews have a number of advantages and disadvantages as a research method. They may feel intuitively 'familiar' to you because you use them in your everyday social work practice. You are more likely to have transferable skills and experience than with other research methods and are more likely to feel confident using them. Interviews enable you to access people's feelings and attitudes and allow you to probe for more detailed responses. Consequently, they provide richer and more in-depth data. They enable you to follow up interesting responses in ways that are not possible using other methods such as questionnaires and documentary analysis. If you are interested in participants' individual views and experiences, interviews are more likely to provide a setting that is conducive to openness than a focus group.

However, it is time-consuming to access participants, arrange a suitable time and venue and to transcribe interviews. Developing an interview schedule requires time and effort and will usually require a number of drafts. Although the data you obtain are richer and more detailed, this usually makes them more difficult to analyse than more quantitative methods such as questionnaires.

Conducting the interview

Before the interview make a checklist of essential items to take, such as your interview schedule, consent forms and information sheets and a recorder (if appropriate) with spare tapes and batteries. If possible, learn your interview schedule and at least rehearse the opening sequence.

When you begin the interview remind them of who you are and the purpose of your research. Make it clear that they do not have to answer any questions that they do not want to. Participants may ask about the limits of confidentiality so ensure you are clear about your position and do not promise anything that you cannot deliver.

During the interview work to build up rapport and trust with the participant. Listen to what they say and follow up when unclear. Have breaks if necessary, but be guided by the participant.

After the interview thank the participant for their time, leave time to write up notes and consider sending the participant a copy. Ensure that you store the data ethically.

Recording the interview

There are a number of advantages to recording your interviews. You can give your participant your full attention rather than dividing it between writing and listening. You will have a full record of the interview that you can make notes from and come back to. This is particularly important if a subsequent interview echoes unexpected themes from an earlier interview that are worth following up. However, your participant might be uncomfortable with recording or might be more wary of being open and honest.

The two options for recording your interviews are video or audio recording. Video recording captures non-verbal communication but is rarely used because it is so intrusive. Audio recording is generally regarded as good enough without being too disruptive. You can use either tape or digital audio recording. The advantages of digital recording are better sound quality because of reduced background noise and playback while transcribing can be more easily controlled. Although more expensive than tape recorders, digital recorders are considerably more affordable than they have previously been. If recording, consider obtaining an external microphone. They are usually better quality that the internal microphone and particularly important if using a tape recorder rather than a digital recorder because they significantly cut down background noise.

Transcribing audio recording of interviews

Transcribing audio recordings of interviews is a time-consuming process. One hour of interview can take 2–6 hours to transcribe and the transcript from a one-hour interview can be 20–40 pages (Boyatzis, 1998). Although it may seem like just a boring administrative task, it is far more than that. While you are listening to the recording, you are starting to analyse your data and see patterns in what was said. You will have begun this process during the interview itself as you tried to make sense of what the participant was saying. Transcribing provides a useful opportunity to continue this analysis before you begin the formal process of data analysis (see Chapter 7 for a detailed discussion of data analysis).

Transcripts should have double line spacing and a wide margin for adding coding and other notes. It can be helpful to include line numbering on your transcripts. In Microsoft Word 2003, line numbering can be turned on by selecting 'file' then 'page setup', choosing the 'layout' tab and then clicking the 'line numbers' box. In Microsoft Word 2007, simply select 'page layout' then 'line numbers'.

Ethical data management

You have a duty to ensure that participants' information is kept safe in a locked or otherwise secured location. For example, transcripts held as a computer file should be password protected. It is good practice to record background information about participants on a personal details form that is kept separate from the interview transcript. The personal details form and the interview transcript are linked by a key in which each participant is given a number. This number is recorded on the transcript and the two sets of documents are kept separately, so that if another party should gain unauthorised access to the transcripts, they will not know the identity of the participant.

C H A P T E R   S U M M A R Y

This chapter has introduced you to the key feature of interviews as a research method. You have considered when it would be most appropriate to use interviews compared to alternative approaches such as questionnaires, focus groups and documentary analysis. After studying the different types of interview, you examined some of the key issues around recruiting and selecting participants and applied this to a student case study.

This chapter also looked at how to develop an interview schedule and understand the range of interview questions that is available to you. You reviewed the functions of different types of question, paying particular attention to questions to avoid. You examined an example of an interview schedule developed for the case study and the rationale for the question content and sequence used. A learning point from this chapter has been the importance of preparation, as careful thought at the early stages can save valuable time in the later stages.

Despite the challenges involved, interviewing is a popular and rewarding research method. It enables you to gain rich and complex data about people's knowledge, experiences, views and attitudes. You have seen in this chapter that careful preparation can avoid the common pitfalls and help you to produce a research project that is well-designed, interesting and useful.

Kvale, S and Brinkmann, S (2008) *Interviews: Learning the craft of qualitative research interviewing*, 2nd edition. London: Sage.
The second edition of a classic text on interviews, which places interviewing firmly within the qualitative tradition. Chapter 7 provides a practical overview of the interview process, while the early chapters address key theoretical issues.

Mason, J (2002) *Qualitative researching.* 2nd edition. London: Sage.
A solid and well-written textbook that combines practical considerations with detailed consideration of theoretical and methodological issues. Chapter 4 on qualitative interviewing is very clear and helpful.

Chapter 4
Focus groups

Introduction

This is the second of four chapters that will introduce you to commonly used research methods and will provide an overview of how focus groups can be used effectively. Focus groups have entered the popular imagination following their controversial use in the early years of the New Labour government (Barbour and Kitzinger, 1999). Although group interviews have a long history in market research and were used to evaluate propaganda during the Second World War, it is only relatively recently that focus groups have become a popular and respected research method in the social sciences (Morgan, 1997).

Focus groups are versatile and have been used for a wide range of topics. For example, focus groups have been used to research infertility in British South Asian communities (Culley, et al., 2007), children's experiences of mental health services (Day, et al., 2006), women's health in rural India (Vissandjée, et al., 2002), female genital mutilation in Switzerland (Thierfelder, et al., 2005), and access to out-of-hours health services by members of the Vietnamese community in London (Free, et al., 1999).

Defining focus groups

A focus group is a group of individuals selected to provide their opinions on a defined subject, facilitated by a moderator who aims to create an open and relaxed environment and promote interaction between participants. Rather than an interview with a number of participants giving their views, focus groups enable discussion between participants (Kitzinger, 1994). Such discussions can enable participants to explore and challenge each other's views and can result in people clarifying and changing their views.

Combining focus groups with other research methods

Focus groups are often used on their own, but can be combined with other research methods such as surveys or interviews (Morgan, 1993, 1997). Focus groups can be used before a survey to provide an overview and test the range of opinions which will be used in questionnaire construction. For example, the Scottish Executive used focus groups to develop a national survey for people from minority ethnic communities (Scottish Executive, 2003).

Interviews can be used in conjunction with focus groups where participants may disclose more sensitive information than they would in a group setting. While focus groups are effective in accessing shared, public knowledge, interviews are fruitful for more personal, biographical information. For research topics that require both forms of knowledge, combining both methods can be productive.

RESEARCH SUMMARY

Combining focus groups and interviews

Michell (1999) conducted a longitudinal study of teenage lifestyles that followed a cohort of 11- and 12-year-olds over time. She sought to understand how changing peer group structures influenced health behaviours. She used a combination of focus groups and interviews to examine teenage relationships, particularly the 'pecking order' in peer relationships.

She found that there were three identifiable groups: 'top' or popular girls, 'middle' girls and marginalised or 'bottom' girls. One of the most interesting insights was the difference between the data revealed in the focus groups compared to the interviews. For 'top' and 'middle' girls, there was little difference between what they said in the focus groups and what they said in the interviews. For marginalised or 'bottom' girls, the picture was quite different. While 'top' and 'middle' girls acknowledged their own status

→

RESEARCH SUMMARY *continued*

in the focus groups, 'bottom' girls did not and were often quieter and sometimes silent. 'Bottom' girls only acknowledged their status in individual interviews and discussed their difficulties in school and often at home.

This difference was only noted in 'low-status' girls. By contrast, Michell found that 'low-status' boys responded in focus groups and interviews in similar ways. She described them as either silent or at best monosyllabic in both settings or were silly and disruptive, relating wildly implausible anecdotes about violence and drug use, etc. (Michell, 1999, p46).

This interesting study provides a useful insight into the limitations of focus groups for subjects that require participants to discuss both public, shared knowledge and personal, biographical information. Combining both methods enabled the researcher to access both forms of knowledge successfully.

Advantages of focus groups

Focus groups enable you to gain a range of opinions about a topic in a fairly easy and reliable way. They can produce significant amounts of data focused on a specific topic and are less time-consuming than interviews. They provide an opportunity for participants to express a range of opinions and challenge and interact with one another in an open environment. Participants can explore and develop their opinions through interactions with others and provide insights into complex behaviours. Finally, they are more accessible than other research methods for people with literacy difficulties (Owen, 2001) or for people who do not have English as a first language (Barbour and Kitzinger, 1999).

Disadvantages of focus groups

Arranging times and venues for a group of people to meet can be complex and demanding, requiring you to engage in considerable negotiation and coordination. Some group members may feel unable to voice their opinions because they feel less confident, less powerful or feel their opinions may be unacceptable to other group members. Recruiting group members from similar backgrounds and a skilled moderator can significantly reduce these risks. The nature of the group context may mean participants do not discuss personal experiences and histories in as much depth or detail as individual interviews (Michell, 1999; Morgan, 1997). Recording and transcribing can be time-consuming and complex, e.g. identifying the contribution of different participants from an audio tape when they have similar voices. Finally, focus groups offer less control over the discussion than an interview.

When not to use focus groups

There are a number of circumstances when focus groups are best avoided:

- when boundary issues may become too complex, e.g. participants have complex relationships with each other that involve potential role conflicts;

- where you are seeking to learn about the individual history and biography of participants (Morgan, 1997, Michell, 1999);

- where you are seeking to make statistical generalisations about a wider population;

- where it would be extremely difficult to bring participants together at a certain time and venue.

Finally, if you are relatively new to research, avoid using focus group to discuss issues that are likely to be very distressing to participants. Focus groups have been successfully used for sensitive topics (Farquhar with Das, 1999; Zeller, 1993), but require considerable experience and skills in moderation.

Selecting and recruiting participants

There is considerable debate about the 'ideal' size for a focus group. Although groups of 8–12 are thought desirable for market research purposes, social research usually uses smaller group sizes, often 6–8 participants (Barbour and Kitzinger, 1999; Krueger and Casey, 2000). It can also depend upon how aware the participants are of the topic – larger groups are necessary when participants have low levels of awareness, while smaller groups enable highly aware participants to discuss the topic in detail (Morgan, 1997).

Large groups can be particularly problematic because, if people don't feel they have the chance to speak, they may be tempted to talk to the person next to them. Valuable data can be lost, particularly if the recording is unclear because both conversations have been picked up.

You should allow for some to drop out (usually 10–20 per cent), although occasionally participants may bring along other people to join in. Although this can be advantageous, you need to consider whether additional people will fit your selection criteria and affect the group dynamics, e.g. making the group too large.

When deciding how many focus groups to conduct, the general consensus for large-scale projects is that it is best to plan three or four focus groups with any one type of participant, i.e. three different groups of social workers (Morgan, 1997, 1998; Krueger and Casey, 2000). Once you've done this, determine if you have reached 'saturation', which is when you are not getting any new ideas from further groups.

Student research is more likely to consist of one or two focus groups, though you need to consult your university supervisor or tutor for their requirements. This is usually sufficient to produce a considerable amount of useful and stimulating data to analyse.

'Naturally occurring' and 'stranger' groups

There are two types of focus group, a 'naturally occurring' group and a 'stranger' group. The naturally occurring group comprises participants who know each other in another role, such as a work team or support group. The stranger or assembled group comprises people who do not know each other but have a similar background or similar experiences. Neither is regarded as being 'better' than the other and your choice depends upon your research.

Participants are more likely to talk more easily in naturally occurring groups and require less time to warm up. However, the challenge for the moderator is to ensure that participants do not become distracted by issues that are not relevant to the research question, such as everyday work issues.

A potential issue when using naturally occurring groups is the possibility of 'group-think', although this can occur in any group. This is the tendency for dissenters in groups to suppress their opinions and for the group to quickly reach a consensus without critically considering the alternatives to avoid conflict (Janis, 1982; Morgan, 1997). This can be challenged and explored by a sensitive moderator and can lead to rich and interesting data.

A discussion about the nature of the boundaries is important for all focus groups but is particularly important for naturally occurring groups. This should include whether your findings will be shared with participants and other parties as well as the disclosure of dangerous practice or risks to other people.

If your research focuses on the 'taken for granted' assumptions underlying a topic, a stranger group may have the advantage that participants are likely to spend more time explaining their reasoning (Morgan, 1998). Stranger groups are popular in market research for this reason, while naturally occurring groups are more common in student research.

Recruiting and selecting participants

Participants for a natural group can be recruited in a number of ways. One of the easiest ways to recruit is to use existing networks, e.g. designing a poster or e-mail to be distributed, being invited to meetings to explain your research. Asking a key figure to distribute your information can be effective, but you need to be careful that participants do not feel under pressure to participate. Try to personalise the invitation as much as possible so as to maximise the likelihood of people participating. Some funded research projects offer incentives such as gift tokens, but providing refreshments and food can be equally successful.

When selecting your participants, your aim is to minimise recruitment bias rather than achieve generalisability (Curtis and Redmond, 2007). Recruitment bias occurs when you select a group that do not reflect the diversity of potential participants. For example, if you are conducting a focus group evaluating a service and approach the manager for details of potential participants, you are likely to receive a list of service users who feel positively about the service. It is difficult to eliminate this entirely; for example, a poster invitation will still attract people who normally get involved in such activities. If possible, introduce an element of randomisation, such as obtaining a list of potential participants and select names at random to approach. Whatever approach you use, be clear about it when writing up your dissertation and discuss the strengths and weaknesses of your approach.

Homogeneous or heterogeneous group?

Although there is debate whether focus groups should be homogeneous (similar) or heterogeneous (dissimilar), most researchers prefer a homogeneous group who share a background or experiences that are the focus of the discussion (Vaughn, et al., 1996; Morgan, 1998). Having a homogeneous group is advantageous because it can help ensure that participants feel able to speak freely and lead to data that is more straightforward to analyse (Krueger and Casey, 2000). Heterogeneous groups are particularly problematic where there are power differentials between participants because apparent consensus may not reflect the real views of all members (Happel, 2007; Krueger and Casey, 2000).

Media portrayals of focus groups often present a misleading picture of a group of different participants selected to represent particular 'segments' of the population, e.g. the token 'white housewife from Middle England', the token 'young Black student', and so on. For your research project, do not try to assemble a group because you believe they will be 'representative' of a particular population, e.g. having a 'representative' service user or social worker. Adopting this approach in user involvement is tokenism, adopting it in research is to misunderstand the nature of focus groups and what can be learnt from them. If you are seeking to be able to generalise statistical findings to a much wider population, a more quantitative approach such as surveys with a larger sample size using the relevant statistical tests is necessary.

If participants are selected to be placed in groups of similar people, known as 'segmenting', the most common categories in large-scale research projects are gender, race, age and social class (Morgan, 1997). For social work students, the categories are more likely to be related to role, e.g. service users, local authority social workers, health professionals, though the previously mentioned factors should also be considered where relevant.

Consequently, if you want to use more than one group, e.g. professionals and service users, hold separate group meetings because participants will feel freer to share their views. If you want to see how views from the two groups interact, this can be achieved by sharing the views of one group with the other group, e.g. sharing the views of the service user group with the professional group and vice versa.

Planning your focus group

There are a number of issues to bear in mind when planning your focus group. Consider when it would be most convenient for participants to meet, including lunch-time and evenings. If participants already know each other, ask whether there is a time when they meet regularly. For example, if a team meet fortnightly on Wednesday mornings, ask whether the focus group could be held in one of the alternate Wednes-days. However, avoid trying to run a focus group after an existing meeting simply because participants are in the same place. They are likely to be tired and unwilling to spend another two hours in a focus group.

Ensure that the venue is accessible by transport and for participants with disabilities. Where participants do not have English as a first language, consider arrangements for interpreters. Make sure that your group is culturally sensitive, e.g. consider single-gender groups with matched moderator, dietary requirements (Cully, et al., 2007). If your participants are professionals and you are holding the focus group at their place of work, there is a risk that participants may be disturbed by colleagues bringing in messages. Asking participants to switch off their mobiles and to make arrangements for other staff to come in only in emergencies can send a clear message that the group is important. Ensure that you provide refreshments and consider offering food as this can be a significant incentive.

Most focus groups last for two hours in total, which includes 90 minutes for the main part and 15 minutes before and after for welcoming participants and concluding the meeting (Curtis and Redmond, 2007; Morgan, 1997). Ensure that you tell participants this to avoid confusion and reduce the risk of people leaving early.

CASE STUDY

Planning a focus group
Patrick is on placement in a large, local authority family centre. He is interested in social workers' views on the barriers to fathers being involved in parenting assessments.

He decided that a focus group would be a good research method because it would enable him to hear a range of views and allow participants to interact with each other and challenge each other's views. His focus was on participants' professional experience rather than their personal biographies as the latter would take much longer to conduct interviews that would produce a similar amount of data. The disadvantages are that it can be difficult to arrange for a group of people to meet, the risk of groupthink and the possibility that some group members do not feel able to express their opinions.

Patrick considered how to select his participants and how many focus groups to run. There are ten full- and part-time staff members in the team, a manager and a deputy manager. Eight staff members were interested in being involved and Patrick decided against involving the manager and deputy manager because the power differential might make it difficult for participants to speak openly.

$\rightarrow$

He contacted a neighbouring family centre and managed to recruit eight staff members, which would enable him to run two focus groups. He decided that each team would involve a mixture of staff from each family centre to reduce the risk of groupthink and a group of eight would enable a few participants to drop out on the day and the group would still be viable. It would also leave other staff members who could field telephone calls while the focus group was on.

Developing a discussion guide

A discussion guide is a list of topics or questions that you produce for yourself as the moderator to guide the conversation. Assuming a two-hour focus group, it is realistic to ask 8–12 questions, depending upon the type of question (Krueger and Casey, 2000). The group nature of the discussions means that fewer questions are asked than in individual interviews.

A discussion guide should have a clear structure and will include a range of different types of question:

1. *Introduction*   Introduce yourself and thank participants for coming. Summarise your research topic briefly and discuss confidentiality and recording. Remind participants of when it will finish and agree ground rules. Morgan (1997) suggests:
   - only one person speaking at a time;
   - no side conversations among neighbours;
   - everyone participating with no one dominating;
   Keep it as brief as possible.

2. *Warm-up questions*   These aim to help participants feel comfortable with speaking in the group and are usually short, factual questions that every participant responds to. Ensuring that everyone makes an initial statement can also reduce the risk of groupthink (Morgan, 1997).

3. *Introductory questions*   These introduce the topic and provide a context, encouraging participants to think about the key topics.

4. *Key questions*   These are the principal questions that directly address your research question. Up to half of the questions will be in this category so ensure that you leave sufficient time for these to be addressed in detail.

5. *Closing questions*   These enable the moderator to check understanding of what has been said, enable participants to provide a summary view and provide an opportunity for any issues not discussed to be addressed. Krueger and Casey (2000) identify three questions in this category:
   - *the 'all things considered' question* – used to clarify the final position of participants on the topics discussed and their relative importance, for example: 'All things considered, what is the most important issue we have discussed here today?' This is particularly important if participants have changed their views

and if they have discussed relatively minor issues more frequently than more important ones;
- *the summary question* – the moderator attempts to summarise the discussion and asks whether it is a fair synopsis;
- *the final question* – having summarised the discussion, the moderator asks whether anything has been overlooked or whether participants want to add anything that they haven't previously said. Ask this with ten minutes left rather than at the very end, when participants may want to finish on time.

Morgan (1997) uses the analogy of a funnel to describe the process of each focus group starting with a less structured general discussion leading to a more structured discussion of specific topics. This allows the first part of the group to concentrate on participants' own perspectives of the topic and the second part to focus on the interviewer's specific interests in the topic (Morgan, 1997).

Organising pilot focus groups is more difficult than pilot interviews, but you can get feedback that can significantly improve your discussion guide. The two best stages at which to involve other people are the initial stage of generating possible questions and at the final stage of developing your discussion guide.

At the initial stage, arrange a short meeting with a few interested people to generate possible research questions. Ideally, this would include at least one person who would fit the criteria for joining your focus group but who will not be participating. You could also involve your practice assessor, placement colleagues and fellow students.

Once you have generated a range of possible questions in the group, arrange another time to meet and take these questions away to work on them on your own. Review them and discard any that are clearly not relevant. Then divide them into two groups, 'need to know' and 'nice to know' (Krueger and Casey, 2000). The former questions are vital to answering your research question while the latter are questions that you are simply curious about. Be honest and ruthless about this and you will probably be surprised by how many fall into the latter category.

One of the temptations in research is 'mission creep', when you become tempted to ask additional questions outside of your initial research question simply because they sound interesting. Material that you gather from 'nice to know' questions will probably never be analysed and make it into your research project. If it does, your dissertation may become confusing and disjointed because you are moving outside your research question.

Once you have decided your core questions, start developing questions in draft form. Questions should be:

- **Specific** Avoid questions that can lead to vague generalisations. Participants provide better quality data when they are asked about issues rooted in their own concrete experience. For example, do not ask 'How does society view fathers?' Instead, invite them to think back to their own experiences and ask them about their own impressions.

- *Clear* Try your questions out on colleagues to test whether they are clear. Avoid asking 'why' questions because participants are likely to give sanitised rationalisations of complex decisions often made on the basis of impulse, habit, tradition or other non-rational processes (Krueger and Casey, 2000). The 'why do you want to become a social worker?' question much cherished by social work admissions panels may illustrate this for you.

- *Conversational* Once you are involved in undertaking research, it is tempting to use academic language to phrase questions. This can make questions impenetrable to participants and increase the risk you will stumble over your words. Rather than ask 'What potential barriers can you identify that would impede a father's participation in the assessment process?' ask 'What are the barriers to fathers being involved in assessment?'

- *Non-confrontational* Participants may become defensive and provide inauthentic responses if they feel criticised. It may be necessary to ask difficult questions, but careful phrasing can make this easier. Difficult questions are best asked towards the end of the group meeting because participants will have had more opportunity to become comfortable with the group. If participants then become defensive or do not wish to continue, you will have minimised the amount of data that will be lost.

CASE STUDY

Discussion Guide
Patrick developed his discussion guide by involving his practice assessor and a staff member from another team to generate some ideas for questions. Using a flipchart and pen, they spent 30 minutes generating as many questions as possible. He took these questions away and redrafted them, ensuring they were in the right sequence. He took them back to his practice assessor and colleague and they provided useful feedback. His discussion guide is given in Figure 4.1.

Role of the group moderator

The role of the moderator is to create an open and relaxed environment and promote interaction between participants. Participants can have different levels of involvement depending upon their relationship with the topic being discussed. Participants with little interest in the topic may show low involvement, while others are very interested and may control the discussion (Morgan, 1997). The aim is to promote the involvement of all participants without allowing particular individuals to dominate.

Having a colleague or fellow student who can assist you is essential. As well as helping you to welcome participants and other practical support, they can take notes, as it is virtually impossible to moderate well and take notes simultaneously. Although you are likely to be recording the group, it can be difficult to distinguish which participant is speaking when you are reviewing the tape afterwards, particularly if participants have

Introduction	Introduce yourself and thank participants for coming. Summarise your research topic briefly and discuss confidentiality and recording. Remind them of the information sheet they have already received, including arrangements around confidentiality. Discuss consent form, participant to sign. Remind participants that they can withdraw at any point and that it is a two-hour focus group. Discuss and agree ground rules.
'Warm-up' questions	*Please tell us your name and tell us briefly what you do for fun.* (Total 15–20 minutes) (Rationale: The group already know each other and this exercise relaxes people and ensures that everyone speaks in the group about a non-threatening subject.)
Introductory questions	*Think back to when you first started undertaking assessments with families. What were your first impressions of fathers? Write your thoughts on a piece of paper and we can then share them as a group.* (Total 25–35 minutes) (Rationale: This exercise gives the message to participants that you are interested in their experiences rather than abstract generalisations. Writing it on a piece of paper counteracts the effects of groupthink as it establishes that everyone has their own view and participants are more likely to share material that they have written down. Asking about their views in the past is less threatening and highlights that views often change over time. Adopting the funnel approach, this question is very open and focused upon participants' experiences and views while the following section is focused upon the researcher's specific interests (Morgan, 1997).)
Key questions	*What are the positive aspects of fathers being involved in assessments?* *What are the less positive aspects?* *What are the barriers to fathers being involved?* *How can those barriers be addressed?* (Total 30–40 minutes) (Rationale: Asking a positive question before a negative question makes it less threatening, while leaving potentially challenging questions until the end minimises the data lost if participants do not respond or become defensive.)
Closing questions	*All things considered, what are the most important barriers to fathers being involved in assessments?* *Is there anything we have missed? Is there anything that you came wanting to say that you didn't get a chance to say yet?* (Total 10 minutes) (Rationale: Enables participants to prioritise the issues discussed and provides an opportunity to discuss any issues not already addressed.)

Figure 4.1 Discussion guide

similar voices. Consequently, your colleague or fellow student should concentrate on recording the order of participants' contributions and brief notes of what was said. If your tape recorder fails, these notes will prevent total catastrophe.

A second person to assist you can prove invaluable, especially if participants unexpectedly bring children or other adults who have accompanied them to the venue. A debriefing session with your assistant moderator(s) afterwards with the tape recorder still running can provide a valuable addition to your notes. Your debriefing should include your thoughts on the interaction between participants as well as the ideas discussed.

Managing the group

Moderating the group is about ensuring that the discussion is open and relaxed while addressing the research question, which can be a delicate balancing act. Try to follow the discussion guide as closely as possible, but do not feel that you have to follow it rigidly. If new issues arise, feel free to explore these if they are likely to provide useful data, but do not feel that you have to let the conversation wander into irrelevant areas.

It is important to keep in mind that a focus group is not a therapy or support group. It is common for participants to enjoy focus groups and this is desirable to give participants something back for the time they have invested and to encourage participation. However, always remember that the purpose is for you to gather data for your research project.

If you are new to focus groups, you will be relieved when participants start talking but you need to continually monitor that they are directly responding to the question. It is all too easy for groups to become sidetracked with issues that are important to them but are not relevant to the research.

CASE STUDY *continued*

It is the day of Patrick's first focus group and one person is off ill and another has to go to court. This still leaves six people and Patrick has decided to go ahead. A colleague has agreed to act as assistant moderator, taking notes.

The group starts well, with participants writing down and then discussing their first impressions of working with fathers. When Patrick asks them about the positive aspects of engaging fathers, one participant states they are already overworked, particularly as there is an unfilled vacancy. There is general unrest in the group and one participant starts whispering to another. The conversation turns to feeling overworked and undervalued in the service.

ACTIVITY 4.1

How can Patrick respond in his role as moderator?

Comment

The risk is that the discussion is likely to get sidetracked into a general discussion about staff shortages and the additional work pressures this causes. While this is important to the team, it is not productive for the research question.

If participants become sidetracked with an issue that they feel is important for them but which is tangential to your topic, you need to bring them back to the research question(s). It is important to do this sensitively so participants do not feel censured. For example, you could say 'That's an important topic, but I would like to hear more about...' If participants continue, it is important to persist, for example saying: 'Perhaps we can come back to that later, but X made an interesting point and I would like to hear more about...'

When groups get sidetracked by other issues, one thing to consider is whether the question is quite difficult or challenging for participants and they are avoiding responding to it. If the group continues to get sidetracked, it can be helpful to ask directly whether the question is difficult to respond to. Expressing this openly encourages participants to either address the question directly or to explore the reasons why it might be a difficult topic to talk about. Either way, it will produce useful data that is relevant to the research question.

Recording and transcribing

Video recording would be ideal from a data-gathering perspective, but is likely to be too intrusive for participants and the equipment is unlikely to be available. Audio recording is the most common compromise, enabling you to keep a recording while not being too intrusive.

Check your equipment beforehand and keep spare batteries and tapes. Most tape and digital recorders have different microphone settings for recording individual interviews and meetings because the acoustics are different. Make sure to select the right setting and consider obtaining a separate microphone for recording meetings. You have worked hard to organise the focus group so ensure you are not let down by technical difficulties.

Krueger (1994) identifies a range of choices when writing up your recordings depending upon the rigour of your analysis and the time you have available:

- *A full transcript* A verbatim transcript is produced and used alongside notes taken during the focus group and afterwards. For some forms of analysis, e.g. conversational analysis, transcripts should include every aspect of the conversation, including pauses and all verbal communication.

- *Tape-based analysis and shortened transcript* A transcript is produced, but it covers the points made rather than being a verbatim account.

- *Note-based analysis*   This relies mainly on notes, a debriefing session and summary comments made at end of the focus group. The session is taped but the tape is only used to verify specific quotes.

- *Memory-based analysis*   Notes can be consulted but most of the write-up is based upon recall.

Most student research uses tape-based or note-based analysis, but this depends upon the requirements of your university and the research approach you have chosen. Your approach also depends upon whether you are using focus groups as a research method in its own right or as a preliminary or exploratory measure for other research methods, such as surveys (Curtis and Redmond, 2007).

Once you have written up your data, it is vital that you keep back-up copies in several places. These need to be password protected to ensure confidentiality. The data analysis process usually involves you cutting and pasting the data into categories or themes and it is all too easy to find that you have cut and pasted the only copy of a transcript.

Data analysis issues

The general process of analysing qualitative data will be discussed in Chapter 7 so the discussion here will be limited to issues that are specific to focus groups.

When analysing focus group data, do not assume that the important subjects are the ones that get talked about most frequently (Krueger and Casey, 2000). One of the advantages of concluding questions such as 'all things considered...?' is that it requires participants to identify the most important issues explicitly. Similarly, it is important to give attention to the personal context that participants use in giving their responses to the topics (Merton, et al., 1990; Green and Hart, 1999).

Sim (1998) identifies three issues concerning the use of focus group data:

- The data you obtain relate to a group rather than to a collection of separate individuals. If a focus group arrives at an apparent consensus, it is difficult to conclude that individual participants hold this view. Group interactions are complex and can lead to individual participants apparently agreeing with a view that they do not privately hold.

- Similarly, it is problematic to measure strength of opinion in a group in the same ways as in individual surveys. While particular views may be present or absent across different focus groups, the relative strength of opinion is difficult to compare.

- Attempting to make generalisations based upon focus group data is misguided, e.g. concluding that the opinions expressed by a particular group of social workers can be taken as representative of social workers as a profession.

C H A P T E R   S U M M A R Y

Focus groups are an increasingly popular research method that has been used to study a wide range of issues. They can be used as a stand-alone method or combined with other research methods such as interviews or surveys.

Focus groups have a range of advantages and disadvantages. They enable you to gain a range of opinions in a fairly easy and reliable way and can produce significant amounts of data focused on a specific topic. They are less time-consuming than interviews and are more accessible than other research methods for people with literacy difficulties, for people whose first language is not English and for traditionally marginalised groups. However, they can be difficult to arrange and recording and transcribing can be complex and time-consuming.

Focus groups can either be naturally occurring groups or stranger groups. Each has their strengths and weaknesses and neither is inherently better. Focus groups in social research tend to be smaller than in market research, often involving 6–8 participants. While large-scale studies involve three or more focus groups per category of participant to exhaust a topic, student research commonly involves one or two groups.

Different methods of recording focus groups and writing up your data were examined. Analysing the data you gather in your focus groups will be discussed in depth in Chapter 7, but some of the issues specific to focus groups were outlined. These include limitations on attempts to measure the opinions of individual group members, strength of opinion and generalisations to wider populations.

FURTHER READING

Barbour, RS and Kitzinger, J (eds) (1999) *Developing focus group research: Politics, theory and practice.* London: Sage.
Excellent edited collection discussing specific issues about the use of focus groups.

Krueger, RA and Casey, MA (2000) *Focus groups.* 3rd edition. Thousand Oaks, CA: Sage.
An excellent introductory text giving sound, practical advice.

Morgan, DL (1997) *Focus groups as qualitative research.* 2nd edition. London: Sage.
Another good introductory text, quite short but covers the major topics.

Sim, J (1998) Collecting and analysing qualitative data: Issues raised by the focus group. *Journal of Advanced Nursing*, 28 (2): 345–52.
A helpful article about data analysis issues for focus groups.

Chapter 5
Questionnaires

ACHIEVING A SOCIAL WORK DEGREE

This chapter will help you to meet the following standards as set out by the Quality Assurance Agency (2008) Subject Benchmark Statement for the social work degree:

- The critical application of research knowledge from the social and human sciences, and from social work (and closely related domains) to inform understanding and to underpin action, reflection and evaluation (4.2).
- Acquire and apply the habits of critical reflection, self-evaluation and consultation, and make appropriate use of research in decision-making about practice and in the evaluation of outcomes (4.7).
- Research-based concepts and critical explanations from social work theory and other disciplines that contribute to the knowledge base of social work, including their distinctive epistemological status and application to practice (5.1.4).
- Knowledge and critical appraisal of relevant social research and evaluation methodologies, and the evidence base for social work (5.1.4).
- Use research critically and effectively to sustain and develop...practice (5.8).
- Demonstrate sufficient familiarity with statistical techniques to enable effective use of research in practice (5.9).
- An ability to use research and enquiry techniques with reflective awareness, to collect, analyse and interpret relevant information (7.3).

Introduction

This is the third of four chapters that will introduce you to commonly used research methods and will provide an overview of how questionnaires can be used effectively. Questionnaires are a popular and widely-used research method, which is at least partly because we are familiar with their use in everyday life and with the underlying principle of considering information that has been obtained from a sample of people to be representative of a much larger group of people.

Questionnaires originate from the survey tradition, which has a long history in the social sciences. The terms 'questionnaire' and 'survey' are often used interchange-ably. *Surveys* are used to study large groups or populations, usually using a standardised, quantitative approach to identify beliefs, attitudes, behaviour and other characteristics. *Questionnaires* form a key research method for collecting survey data, but surveys can use a range of methods, such as highly structured, face-to-face or telephone interviews. Consequently, surveys are an overall research design, while questionnaires are one of the research methods used within surveys.

The long tradition of survey research has led to a considerable amount of rules and guidance about constructing and administering questionnaires. This can appear daunting for the novice researcher. The chapter aims to address the key issues in questionnaire research to enable you to understand the process and avoid the main pitfalls, with further reading for those wanting more exhaustive guidance.

This chapter will discuss when it is appropriate to use questionnaires compared to other research methods. A five-stage model of developing questionnaire research will be presented, taking you from deciding your research question and design through to analysing the data you have collected. In this process, ethical issues and sampling strategies will be explored and the strengths and limitations of questionnaires will be discussed. Throughout, a case study, exercises and practical tips will be provided to help you to manage your questionnaire research project.

When is it appropriate to use questionnaires?

Questionnaires are most appropriate when you want to collect straightforward information on a relatively well-understood topic from a large number of people. If your topic requires more exploratory research using data that are complex and uncertain from a smaller number of people, more qualitative research methods such as interviews and focus groups may be more appropriate. Consider the following.

ACTIVITY 5.1

Varsha is a final-year student who is interested in her fellow students' experiences of their social work training. She is considering two research questions:

1. Do social work students feel that their social work training is preparing them for professional practice?
2. How do social work students use theory to respond to complex practice situations?

Which question do you think would be more appropriate for using questionnaires?

Comment

The first question can be answered by quantitative data that measures participants' attitudes and beliefs. The second question is more suited to qualitative methods, such as interviews and focus groups, which can provide opportunities for participants to draw upon their experiences of using theory to respond to practice situations.

Questionnaires are most suited to gathering predominantly quantitative data. It is helpful for you to collect some qualitative data, usually through open-ended questions, but this is supplementary to your main quantitative questions. For this reason, questionnaire research is best suited for topics that are relatively well-known and can effectively build upon previous research. Topics that are less known are usually more suited to more exploratory, qualitative research.

One of the most common mistakes made in student research using questionnaires is to include a significant number of open-ended, qualitative questions. This is problematic for two reasons. Firstly, participants are unlikely to fill out the questionnaire completely because they do not want to keep writing long passages. So some questions will be ignored and participants may give up part way through. Secondly, it can be difficult to understand the answers they give as participants may respond to a question in very different ways and there is no opportunity to clarify responses with participants. Unlike other methods such as interviews and focus groups, you have no opportunity to clarify or explore the responses that a participant gives and the result may be significant amounts of missing or confusing data. Consequently, it is best to keep the number of open-ended questions to a minimum (Bryman, 2008).

The most famous example of using open-ended, qualitative questions inappropriately comes from Karl Marx, whose workers' survey (*Enquête Ouvrière*) was a questionnaire sent out to 25,000 French socialists and others. It had 101 questions, finishing with the following question:

> *What is the general, physical, intellectual and moral condition of men and women employed in your trade?* (Bottomore and Rubel, 1963, p218)

Unsurprisingly, there is no record of any questionnaires being returned!

The five stages of completing a questionnaire study

The process of completing a questionnaire study consists of five stages:

1. Deciding your research question and design.
2. Designing your questionnaire, including ethical issues.
3. Sampling.
4. Data collection.
5. Data analysis.

Stage 1 Deciding your research question and design

This stage involves deciding your research question and you may have a specific hypothesis that you wish to test. A *hypothesis* is *a statement about the relationship between two or more variables and predicts an expected outcome* (Hek and Moule,

2006, p58). It is a hunch coming from your reading of the literature, a theory or your own observations and experience and it must be capable of being tested (Nardi, 2006).

As questionnaires are most often and most effectively used in quantitative research, you need to identify the variables that are most relevant to your research question. *Variables* are attributes that can take on different values with different cases and could include your participants' attitudes, beliefs, behaviour, knowledge or some other characteristic. We shall follow through this process with Varsha as she develops her research project.

CASE STUDY

Varsha is interested in using questionnaires to study her fellow students' attitudes towards their professional training. She wants to know whether social work students feel that their training course is preparing them for the realities of working as qualified professionals. She is interested in whether participants' responses differed according to year of study, age, gender and amount of pre-qualifying experience.

ACTIVITY 5.2

In the case study, Varsha may have a hypothesis that older students will report higher levels of confidence in their ability to practise. How might she test this? If she proves her hypothesis, will it prove that older students are more prepared to practise after their training?

Comment

If she includes questions about students' age and scaling questions asking students how confident they feel in their social work practice, she will be able to test this hypothesis. With regard to the second question, remember that Varsha's project is a survey of the *attitudes* of student social workers rather than an observation of their practice. Consequently, proving her hypothesis means that older students are more likely to report feeling confident about being prepared to practise. The question of whether they actually are more prepared for practice is a different question, but this is not the focus of her study.

Operationalisation, validity and reliability

The process of deciding which indicators to use when measuring variables is called *operationalisation*, i.e. how to convert an abstract concept into a quantifiable measure. For example, Varsha wants to measure how confident student social workers feel about their practice and has chosen to use a ratings scale completed by students because it is specific and measurable. She wants to see the relationship between this and the student's year of study, age and gender.

Two key concepts that you need to look at when choosing the indicators that you wish to measure are validity and reliability. *Validity* refers to whether what we are measuring is what we think we are measuring. *Reliability* refers to how consistent or stable a particular measure is. To use an example, imagine that Varsha wants to measure how confident student social workers are and decides that the best way to do this is by measuring their physical height. Since height is not a measurement of confidence, this will not be a valid measure because she will not be measuring what she thinks she is measuring. However, assuming she uses an ordinary tape measure, it could be a reliable measurement in the sense that she will measure students repeatedly and receive the same results. However, if she uses a tape measure made out of elastic, the results will be neither valid nor reliable because she will receive different results at different times.

Stage 2 Developing your questionnaire

The process of developing your questionnaire will require you to think about the layout, the questions that you want to ask and the order in which they appear on the questionnaire. It is generally recognised that having an attractive layout is important to ensuring that you have a good response rate. A poorly designed and visually unappealing questionnaire is more likely to be consigned to the waste paper bin so it is worth investing time in getting it right.

A common student question is how long a should questionnaire be. The golden rule is that questionnaires should *include as many questions as necessary and as few as possible* (Sarantakos, 2005, p242).

ACTIVITY 5.3

Think about your own experiences of filling out questionnaires. What were the best and worst parts? How long were you prepared to spend on completing a questionnaire?

Comment

When thinking about issues of questionnaire length and design, it can be useful to think about what it would be like to be the participant completing it. Most participants are prepared to spend between 5 and 15 minutes to complete a questionnaire. If your questionnaire requires considerably longer, you are likely to find that your response rate is lower and you are more likely to have partially completed questionnaires.

Choosing your questions

When you are thinking of what questions you will include in your questionnaire, begin by generating a range of possible questions. You do this either on your own or preferably with other people who have an interest in your research topic but who are not going to be participants. Review the questions that you generate and discard any that are clearly not relevant.

The next stage is to divide your questions into two groups, 'need to know' and 'nice to know' (Krueger and Casey, 2000). 'Need to know' questions are vital to answering your research question while 'nice to know' questions are ones that you are simply curious about. If you include all of your 'nice to know' questions, your questionnaire will be so long that it is unlikely that many of your participants will ever reach the end. Try to restrict yourself to purely 'need to know' questions and you will maximise the probability of your questionnaire being completed while ensuring that your data are relevant to your research question.

Questions are traditionally divided into closed and open-ended questions. Closed questions provide participants with a fixed number of responses, while open-ended questions allow participants to respond in their own words. On most social work courses, you are encouraged to avoid closed questions and to introduce more open-ended questions into your interactions with service users. This is entirely appropriate, but it is the opposite case for questionnaire research. Closed questions with a fixed number of responses produce quantitative data that are easy to analyse.

Many of the principles of developing questions are similar to those suggested to interviews and focus groups. Ensure that your questions are clear and unambiguous, without confusion and vagueness. Avoid double-barrelled questions, such as 'Did you enjoy your lectures and your practice placement?', because participants may have different responses to different parts of the question and are likely to respond to only one part. Participants provide more reliable responses to questions that relate to their own direct experience rather than more general questions that encourage speculation and generalisations. Questions that require memory recall should be realistic.

It is important to make sure that your questions are not repetitive. It is quite common for the initial drafts of questionnaires to ask the same question in different forms, which is confusing for participants. Language that is particularly emotional or value-laden should be avoided and the use of leading questions, i.e. questions that suggest a particular response should be avoided. It can be difficult to pick these up yourself, so piloting your draft questionnaire is very useful. Ensure that your questions are clear and free from jargon and abbreviations which are likely to antagonise participants, e.g. 'How did your course prepare you to meet Key Roles 2 and 4?' Try your questions out on colleagues, fellow students or friends to test whether they are clear.

Asking 'why' questions is generally discouraged in questionnaire research. 'Why' questions suggest to participants that they should provide a rational response to what might be a decision based upon impulse, habit, tradition or other non-rational process (Krueger and Casey, 2000). If so, participants are likely to provide an intellectual rationalisation that bears little relation to the real process.

Avoid negative questions, particularly double negatives. Participants often accidently read negative questions as positive questions and answer them accordingly, while double negatives are simply confusing.

A final issue is whether you should offer a 'don't know' option. Bryman (2008) argues that this is problematic, particularly when you are asking a question about attitudes. Although there is a possibility that participants will choose it as an easy option, leaving it out would force participants to either select an attitude they do not hold or not answer the question at all.

Deciding question order

It is helpful for participants if you structure the different sections of your questionnaire to flow like a conversation, following a logical order. Move from the familiar to the least familiar to enable participants to begin with what they know best. Similarly, begin with more objective questions and move to more subjective questions as participants become more comfortable. Sensitive questions should be left to later in the questionnaire, but not at the end. As participants can become tired, have fairly straightforward questions at the end, such as participants' age, gender and ethnicity.

Choosing the format for responses

You can choose a number of different formats for how you want participants to respond (Sarantakos, 2005; Sharp, 2009). Whichever response format is used, it is essential to give clear instructions to participants about how questions should be answered.

- *Exact responses* These require a specific answer, e.g. the number of years of social work experience, participants had before starting their degree.

- *Category responses* These require participants to select one response from a list of categories, e.g. experience expressed as 0–2 years, 3–4 years.

- *Dichotomous responses* These are usually in the form of yes/no answers, but could include other dichotomous responses, e.g. male/female.

- *Likert scale questions* Usually require participants to select a response along a sliding scale of agreement. The most common format for a Likert scale is to have two extreme positions divided by a five-point scale, though a seven-point scale can be used to distinguish subtle gradations.

- *Semantic differential scale* Two opposite adjectives are placed on a numerical scale and participants choose which number best represents their view.

- *Graphic scales* Graphic representations, such as faces or ladders, are used to represent participants' attitudes. These are commonly used in learning disability research and can be particularly helpful with children.

- *Constant-sum scales and pie charts* Participants are asked to score two or more alternatives so that the scores add up to a fixed amount or are presented with a blank pie chart and asked to divide it up to represent the relative importance of particular elements.

A key factor in determining what format you wish to use is how you are going to analyse the data afterwards. Consequently, it is worthwhile reading this section alongside Chapter 7, which describes the processes of descriptive statistics that you can use with your data and some of the limitations of particular types of data. If you do not look ahead to how you are going to analyse your data, there is a danger that you will collect data in a form that does not allow you to use the statistical procedures that you want at the analysis stage.

Let us look at Varsha's questionnaire, as shown in Figure 5.1, as an example.

Comment

Varsha's questionnaire uses a wider range of questions than you would normally find, but this is to illustrate the different formats that are available. It is important to have some variety in the types of questions that you ask rather than simply having one type, e.g. yes/no answers.

Is it acceptable to use a previously published questionnaire?

If you can find a suitable published questionnaire that has been developed and validated in previous research studies, then check with your university that you can use it for your research (Fink, 2006). Of course, if your course requires you to design a questionnaire, this will not be appropriate. But it often comes as a surprise to students to find that they may be able to use a standardised questionnaire developed elsewhere. Often this is welcomed because it promotes high-quality research and makes your results more comparable with those found in other research studies.

Ethical issues

There are ethical issues to be addressed when using questionnaires, though they are generally regarded as having lower ethical risks than more intrusive research methods. Unlike interviews and focus groups, questionnaires offer the possibility of anonymity because the researcher may not know the identity of participants, which is a higher level of protection than confidentiality. This makes questionnaires useful for researching sensitive topics because participants are more likely to disclose sensitive material if they can remain anonymous. Promising anonymity is problematic if questionnaires are returned via e-mail as the researcher will usually be able to identify participants, but you will always be able to offer confidentiality.

It is common practice for questionnaires to not require written consent forms, since consent can be implied by participants completing and returning the questionnaire. However, participants do require information about the research, which is normally contained in information sheets or covering letters. You will normally have to go through a university ethics committee or similar research governance process, which usually provide guidance or templates for what information is required.

This questionnaire will ask you about your social work course.

About your course

1. **Which year of the social work degree are you currently in?**

    First   Second   Third

    ☐   ☐   ☐

    1   2   3

2. **Your confidence about specific skills and areas of knowledge**

    Please tick ✓ the box that is closest to your opinion.

I feel confident about...	Strongly agree	Agree	Neither agree nor disagree	Disagree	Strongly disagree
My listening and communication skills	☐	☐	☐	☐	☐
My ability to complete an assessment competently	☐	☐	☐	☐	☐
My advocacy skills	☐	☐	☐	☐	☐
My ability to apply social work theories in practice	☐	☐	☐	☐	☐
My knowledge of the law	☐	☐	☐	☐	☐
Code	*5*	*4*	*3*	*2*	*1*

3. **Overall, how would you rate how confident you feel about your ability to practise social work competently?**

    Please put a number between 1 to 10 in the box (1 = very unconfident, 10 = very confident)

    ☐

    Comment

4. **Overall, to what extent do you agree or disagree that your professional social work degree is preparing you for practice?**

    Please tick ✓ one box only

	Strongly agree	Agree	Neither agree nor disagree	Disagree	Strongly disagree
	☐	☐	☐	☐	☐
Code	*5*	*4*	*3*	*2*	*1*

    →

Figure 5.1 Excerpts from case study questionnaire

Comment

5. **How important have the following parts of your training been to your professional development?**

   You have 100 positive points to divide between the following elements of your course to show how important they are to your professional development. How would you allocate them? *Insert a score against each element, which should add up to 100.*

   Lectures/seminars
   Private study   +
   Placement   + ___
   Total   = 100

6. **Which services do you wish to work in once you have qualified?**

   Please tick one box

   Children and families   ☐   Adult ☐

7. **Which sector do you wish to work in once you have qualified?**

   Please tick one box

   Statutory   ☐
   Voluntary   ☐
   Private sector ☐

About you

This information is collected to see whether there are differences between the views of different people. All information will be kept confidential.

8. **Are you female or male?**

   Please tick ✓ one box only

   Female   Male
   ☐   ☐
   1   2

9. **What was your age at your last birthday?**

   Please write in box   ☐

10. **How many years of social care experience did you have when you started your degree?**

    Please write in box   ☐

Figure 5.1 Excerpts from case study questionnaire (continued)

Stage 3 Sampling

The next stage is to decide how you are going to select your sample. *Sampling* refers to the process of selecting the participants that will be involved in your study. Your sample of participants is chosen from the total possible group of people known as the *population*.

The two main types of sampling are probability and non-probability sampling. *Probability* or *random sampling* uses mathematical techniques based upon probability theory to select research participants who are representative of the overall population. It is the most commonly used sampling approach used in questionnaire research and randomisation increases the likelihood that the results will be generalisable to a wider population. Non-probability sampling is more usually used in qualitative research and is discussed in depth in Chapter 3.

You may think that you have to divide up your sample in certain ways, such as age, gender and ethnicity. It is worthwhile considering whether this is necessary, particularly if the resultant sample size is relatively small. For example, having one or two people from a specific ethnic group is too small to be able to make any worthwhile generalisations. In research, it is always wise to be realistic about what you can claim based upon your evidence and better to understate rather than overstate your case.

Choosing your sample is important, as it will have influence on what data you receive. A famous example is the *Chicago Daily Tribune* erroneously announcing that Republican Thomas Dewey had won the US presidential election in 1948 rather than Democrat Harry Truman. This occurred because the newspaper had seen polls that predicted a Dewey victory but the polls had been conducted using a biased sample. The polls were conducted using fixed quotas from rural and urban populations that had not been updated to reflect the recent move from rural areas into cities. Consequently, they under-represented urban voters who were more likely to vote for Democrat Truman (Andersen and Taylor, 2005, p42).

Bryman (2008) identifies four main types of probability sampling: simple random sampling, systematic sampling, stratified random sampling and multi-stage cluster sampling.

- **Simple random sampling**   This is the most basic form of random sampling, in which cases are selected randomly using random number tables or an online random generator (such as www.randomizer.org). Each unit of the population has an equal chance of being included in the sample and this method eliminates human bias. However, it is only possible if you have a list of all the people in your population, i.e. a sampling frame.

- **Systematic sampling**   This is a variation of the simple random sample in which cases are selected in a systematic way, e.g. choosing every tenth case. It is important to ensure the sampling frame (list of potential participants) is not structured in a way that would make it non-random and, if so, to randomise the order of the list.

- *Stratified random sampling* If there are particular factors that you wish to concentrate upon, you may wish to ensure that the sample ensures sufficient representation. In the case study, Varsha may be interested in whether gender makes a difference in students' attitudes about their professional training. She could establish the overall gender proportions in the social work student group and choose a proportionate sample for each gender. Having established the overall target number of participants for each gender, she would then choose specific participants using simple random sampling or systematic sampling.

- *Multi-stage cluster sampling* When your sample is geographically spread, cluster sampling enables you to group together potential participants. Imagine that Varsha wanted to research social work students across the UK. It would be unrealistic to randomly sample every social work student as that would need students from every university. Instead, cluster sampling would enable her to choose a smaller number of universities through random sampling. She may wish to group the universities further, e.g. choosing regions, and randomly select them within specific regions (Bryman, 2008).

Stage 4 Data collection

Having developed your questionnaire, it is important to pilot it because, unlike interviews or focus groups, you will not have the opportunity to explain ambiguous or unclear questions. Questions that make sense to you may not make sense to your participants and you may find that participants consistently misread questions so these need to be reworded.

Your aim is to maximise your response rate. Having developed a clear and attractive questionnaire, you can improve your response rate by using follow-up letters with additional copies of your questionnaire. This can be fruitful, but do not delay your project too much hoping to receive substantially more. A general rule of thumb is that you will receive about three-quarters of completed questionnaires that you will ever receive within the first three weeks. The final quarter will respond to your reminder letter, but there will come a point when you have to decide to proceed to the next stage.

Stage 5 Analysing your data and presenting your findings

The analysis of your data using descriptive statistics will be discussed in detail in Chapter 7 and the presentation of your findings will be the focus in Chapter 8. It is worthwhile to read this now to ensure you are prepared for the final stages.

Strengths and limitations of questionnaires

Questionnaires have a number of strengths and weaknesses (Sarantakos, 2005; Bryman, 2008).

Strengths

- Questionnaires are relatively inexpensive and quick to administer.

- Participants can respond when it is convenient for them and there is a greater assurance of anonymity.

- There is less opportunity for errors or bias caused by the presence of the interviewer e.g. participants giving answers that are sociably acceptable but not accurate (social desirability bias).

- The questions are asked in a stable and consistent manner, with no interviewer variability.

- They allow greater coverage because participants can be approached more easily and there are no problems around 'non-contacts', where participants are not available at the time (Sarantakos, 2005).

Weaknesses

- Questionnaires do not allow opportunities for probing and clarifying responses with participants or for collecting additional information (e.g. observation) while the questionnaire is being completed.

- The researcher does not have an opportunity to motivate the participant to complete all of the questions or ensure the questions are answered in the correct order, if relevant.

- There are limitations on how long participants are willing to spend on completing a questionnaire.

- Only a very limited number of open questions can be asked because participants do not want to write large amounts.

- They are less appropriate for people with literacy difficulties or for whom English is not a first language.

- The identity of the participant is not known, so the researcher cannot be sure the right person has completed the questionnaire.

C H A P T E R   S U M M A R Y

In this chapter, we have learnt about questionnaires as a research method within the survey tradition. You have been invited to consider which types of research question are appropriate to be addressed using questionnaires. A five-stage model of developing questionnaire research has been presented, taking you from deciding your research question and design through to analysing the data you have collected. In this process, ethical issues and sampling strategies were explored and the strengths and limitations of questionnaires were discussed. Throughout, a case study, exercises and practical tips were provided to help you to manage your questionnaire research project.

FURTHER READING

De Vaus, DA (2002) *Surveys in social research.* 5th edition. London: Routledge.
Fifth edition of a classic text on survey research. Readable and authoritative.

Sapsford, R (2007) *Survey research.* 2nd edition. London: Sage.
Useful and readable text that covers the key issues in survey research.

WEBSITES

The Survey Question Bank (SQB): http://surveynet.essex.ac.uk/sqb/qb/
The Survey Question Bank is part of the Survey Resources Network (**http://surveynet.essex.ac.uk**), an Economic and Social Research Council (ESRC) initiative co-ordinated by the UK Data Archive (UKDA) at the University of Essex.

Chapter 6

Documentary analysis

A C H I E V I N G   A   S O C I A L   W O R K   D E G R E E

This chapter will help you to meet the following standards as set out by the Quality Assurance Agency (2008) Subject Benchmark Statement for the social work degree:

- The critical application of research knowledge from the social and human sciences, and from social work (and closely related domains) to inform understanding and to underpin action, reflection and evaluation (4.2).
- Acquire and apply the habits of critical reflection, self-evaluation and consultation, and make appropriate use of research in decision-making about practice and in the evaluation of outcomes (4.7).
- Research-based concepts and critical explanations from social work theory and other disciplines that contribute to the knowledge base of social work, including their distinctive epistemological status and application to practice (5.1.4).
- Knowledge and critical appraisal of relevant social research and evaluation methodologies, and the evidence base for social work (5.1.4).
- Use research critically and effectively to sustain and develop...practice (5.8).
- Demonstrate sufficient familiarity with statistical techniques to enable effective use of research in practice (5.9).
- An ability to use research and enquiry techniques with reflective awareness, to collect, analyse and interpret relevant information (7.3).

Introduction

This chapter is the last of four chapters on popular research methods and will focus on using documentary analysis for your project. It is one of the lesser known and used social research methods, compared to research methods such as interviews and questionnaires. McCulloch (2004) argues that it was used by Durkheim and was popularised in the 1920s and 1930s by the Chicago School of Sociology before being challenged by quantitative research methods.

Documentary analysis is likely to become more popular in the future because the increasing availability of online documents means that significantly more data is readily available. Indeed, digital archives could revolutionise history as a subject in a way equalled only by the invention of printing (McCulloch, 2004, p41).

This chapter introduces you to a three-stage process of undertaking a documentary analysis, using the example of a case study to illustrate the process. In the case study, content analysis will be used as a popular and straightforward research design. If a more qualitative approach is sought, alternative models of data analysis will be discussed in Chapter 7.

First of all, what do we mean by a 'document'? The question of what constitutes a document is interpreted in an increasingly wide variety of ways, e.g. not just paper documents, but visual data such as photographs and television programmes. Consequently, the term 'text' rather than document has been used to include a wider variety of material (O'Leary, 2004, p177).

The significant growth in online material has provided rich new sources of data. Subject-based discussion groups or bulletin boards provide interesting material but raise new ethical dilemmas. For example, service users and carers use bulletin boards anonymously as a way of accessing support and sharing experiences. Although the information is public and usually anonymous, the individuals cannot be considered to have consented to have their information used for research purposes. These ethical dilemmas are likely to become more acute as more online material becomes available.

Documents are central to the everyday realities of working in the health and social care field and serve many purposes. Legislative and policy statements issued by governmental departments set out the principles and priorities of the current administration and their development is recorded through the parliamentary process. Inquiry reports investigate individual cases where things have gone seriously wrong and make recommendations for the future. Media documents in print, online and in audiovisual forms record events that can shape public opinions about health and social care issues. Local authority documents, such as committee minutes, record key discussions and decisions made about resource allocation and other key matters. Individual case records document events and processes and record decision-making by different agencies. All of these are legitimate sources for documentary analysis.

Documents not only passively record events but can have a profound influence on the ways in which we understand and structure those events. When you go out to conduct an assessment of a service user, it is likely that the agency documentation that you complete will influence how you see the service user, your role and the function of your agency. This too is a legitimate focus for research and can identify implicit beliefs and assumptions contained within documents.

Scott (1990) outlines four criteria for judging documents for research purposes. The first criterion is *authenticity*, which focuses on issues of soundness and authorship. We need to establish the authenticity of the document and the identity of the author. For example, government documents and inquiry reports may be published under the name of a minister or chairperson but may be the work of a team of people (Scott, 1990).

The second criterion is *credibility*, which focuses on sincerity and accuracy. We must consider the extent to which a document is likely to be an undistorted account. No account will be entirely undistorted, because decisions have been made about what to include or what to leave out as well as how the material will be presented. The task is to establish the extent to which the author had a clear interest in presenting material in a certain light. For example, both government policy documents and social work reports share the dual functions of informing readers and also persuading them about the wisdom of the course of action proposed.

The third criterion is *representativeness*, which focuses on the extent to which the documents available are representative of all documents (whether the document is typical of its kind). For historical documents, this can include asking whether some documents survived while others did not. It can also raise issues of power, e.g. when a service user goes to see a psychiatrist, it will usually be the psychiatrist who documents the encounter. Similarly, meetings can involve considerable debate, but the version that is presented in the minutes would usually have precedence.

The final criterion is *meaning*, which focuses on whether the evidence is clear and comprehensible. It is also important to establish whether the meanings contained within a document are literal or whether they are latent (Scott, 1990). Literal meanings are explicit and straightforward, while latent meanings are implicit and require further interpretation.

Your research question and approach will influence how you approach your documents. If your research approach is a traditional, positivist approach, you will view documents as providing straightforward evidence for social phenomena. For example, you may research newspaper articles for evidence of the frequency and severity of attacks on members of the public by people diagnosed with schizophrenia. If your research approach is interpretative, you will view documents as reflecting how social phenomena have been constructed. You would view the same newspaper articles, but you would be interested in how people diagnosed with schizophrenia are portrayed, e.g. whether the language used increases the perceptions of risk of violence.

Common pitfalls

The relatively infrequent use of documentary analysis is at least partly due to the confusion about how to complete such an analysis. One of the most common problems that students experience is confusing a documentary analysis with a literature review. Sometimes students think that they are doing a documentary analysis because they are reviewing the previous academic and practitioner research on their chosen topic. In fact, they are completing a literature review, which is required in every traditional research dissertation (see Chapter 2 for a detailed discussion). This confusion is understandable because students will be analysing documents. However, documentary analysis is used in a more restricted sense.

A literature review is a critical summary of what other researchers have found, i.e. *their* analysis of *their* data. So in your literature review, you are reporting what other people have found. A documentary analysis is *your* analysis of *your* own data in which you are reporting what you have found.

The key to understanding how a documentary analysis differs from a literature review lies in the distinction between primary and secondary sources. A *primary source* is raw data that you have collected yourself to analyse for your research topic while a *secondary source* is someone else's analysed data that would form part of your literature review. An analogy would be if you were studying gender in the paintings of Picasso – the paintings themselves would be primary sources to be analysed while the writings of other commentators would be secondary sources to be discussed in your literature review.

CASE STUDY

Sarah is a student on a mental health placement. She is interested in how the media portray women with a diagnosis of schizophrenia and has decided to use documentary analysis for her research project within a feminist paradigm.

ACTIVITY 6.1

Sarah has the documents listed below. Which documents are included in the literature review and which documents are going to be studied in the documentary analysis?

1. An article from the Times Online about a young woman with a diagnosis of schizophrenia who was involved in a dispute with a neighbour.
2. A book that describes research into how people with mental health problems are portrayed in the media.

Comment

1. The article is a primary source – raw data about how the media portrays people with mental health problems.

2. The book is a secondary source – a developed analysis based upon the author's own research, which Sarah needs to discuss in her literature review.

The distinction between primary and secondary data can occasionally become blurred because it is not only what type of documents you use, but the way in which you use them. For example, if your research project is about how young black men are portrayed in government policy, you would be analysing government policy documents as primary sources but also discussing them in your literature review. However, your main secondary sources are likely to be commentators who present their own analyses of how young black men are viewed within society.

In Chapter 1, we discussed the research process. The traditional research dissertation is structured so that your literature review evaluates what other researchers and commentators have discussed on your topic, i.e. you review the secondary sources. You then present what you found when you analyse your primary sources and compare it with the secondary material. In the example above, this means your literature review discusses what other commentators have said about gender in Picasso's paintings. You would then present your own analysis of gender formed from looking at the paintings and compare it to the previous commentaries. Is there agreement between what you found and what the secondary sources found, or was it different? If so, why do you think this is so? This process will be discussed in more detail in Chapter 8, which focuses on writing up your research project.

CASE STUDY *continued*

Sarah is interested in how the media portrays women with a diagnosis of schizophrenia and has decided to use documentary analysis for several reasons. Firstly, it has lower ethical risks than other methods and usually does not require ethical approval if using publicly available data. Secondly, it does not require her to gain access to participants. Thirdly, it is easy to collect data, especially if using online sources. This enables more data to be collected and more time for analysis. Finally, the data already exists and is not biased by the researcher in the same way that can happen in interviews and focus groups.

The process of conducting a documentary analysis has three stages: firstly, deciding your research question and designing your research; secondly, deciding which documents to analyse and what to include in your sample; thirdly, collecting and analysing your data. These will be discussed in turn.

Stage 1 Deciding your research question and designing your research

Most research methods are located within a particular tradition, e.g. surveys and questionnaires within the quantitative tradition, interviews within the qualitative tradition. Documentary analysis is unusually versatile in that both quantitative and qualitative research designs can be used.

RESEARCH SUMMARY

One of the research studies that Sarah found for her literature review was a study about how people with mental health problems are represented in the media.

The Glasgow Media Group produced a classic study into media portrayals of people with mental health problems (Philo, 1996). In order to identify the dominant messages which are being given out about mental illness across a variety of media, the study included all media content for a period of one month. The sample included television news and press reporting, popular magazines, children's literature, soap operas, films and dramas.

The study yielded a total of 562 items whose content fell into five main categories:

1. *Violence to others.*
2. *Harm to self.*
3. *Prescriptive/advice.*
4. *Criticism of accepted definitions of mental illness.*
5. *'Comic' images.*

→

They found that the category of 'violence to others' was by far the most common, out-weighing the next most common ('advice') by a ratio of almost four to one. They also found that items linking mental illness and violence tended to receive 'headline' treatment, while more sympathetic items were largely 'back page' in their profile, such as problem page letters or health columns. For an excellent update on media representations of mental health, see Clements and Foster (2008).

Having read the Glasgow study, Sarah has decided that content analysis would be a suitable method for her research.

The study uses content analysis, which is one of the most common research designs employed by students using documentary analysis. It is a popular choice at least partly because it provides a relatively straightforward way of making sense of textual data by converting it into a quantifiable form. However, there are a range of different approaches within the qualitative tradition (Miles and Huberman, 1994). These include approaches such as discourse analysis (Parker, 1992; Potter and Wetherell, 1987), narrative analysis (Andrews, et al., 2008; Riessman, 1993, 2007) and semiotics (Saussure, 1983; Barthes, 1972).

What is content analysis? Some definitions

An established definition is that content analysis is *a research technique for the objective, systematic and quantitative description of the manifest content of communication* (Berelson, 1952, p18). As the quote suggests, content analysis uses objective and systematic counting and recording procedures to produce quantitative data about the manifest, i.e. visible content of communication. It is most commonly used in the analysis of mass communication, but it is a versatile research method (Bryman, 2008).

One of the key choices that you must make for your content analysis is the extent to which you will use manifest and latent coding. *Manifest coding* refers to analysing the visible, explicit content of a text, a relatively straightforward process of counting the relative frequency of particular terms. However, it presupposes that different texts use the same or similar terms. *Latent coding* refers to analysing the implicit content of a text and it involves a degree of interpretation to uncover the meanings that lie beneath the actual words in the text.

In the case study, Sarah must make a choice about the extent to which she will use manifest or latent coding.

One of the issues that she wishes to investigate is whether newspapers use discriminatory language when reporting news stories about people diagnosed with schizophrenia. If she wishes to use manifest coding, she would develop a list of specific discriminatory terms that she would look for. If she wishes to use latent coding, she would take into account implied meanings that would suggest that the individual is being viewed negatively even if the article was not explicitly discriminatory.

If Sarah chooses manifest coding, she risks missing news stories where discrimination is present but not explicit. If she chooses latent coding, she risks misinterpreting subtle meanings that are implied but not explicit. Like many research decisions, there is no 'right' answer – she must simply make a decision and give her rationale for it.

Advantages and disadvantages of content analysis

Content analysis has a number of strengths and weaknesses. Content analysis is able to quantify the content of texts in a transparent and clear way (Bryman, 2008; Denscombe, 2007). The procedures are relatively objective and exhibit reliability because they can be replicated by others. It is a flexible method, particularly suited to longitudinal studies which look at phenomena over time (see Clements and Foster, 2008, for a good example). It can reveal hidden aspects of what is being communicated because researchers can code for aspects that are not included in the text, e.g. analysing luxury car adverts for images of people from minority ethnic communities.

Content analysis has been criticised for being a crude instrument because of its tendency to remove text from its context, which risks losing some of its complex and subtle meanings. As a result, it is regarded as being most appropriate when what you are studying is relatively straightforward, clear and observable (Denscombe, 2007). The use of latent coding provides more flexibility and allows data to be viewed in its context, but is controversial because it introduces a level of interpretation. One way in which this can be addressed is by establishing inter-rater reliability through having multiple coders and checking whether different coders identify the same meanings. As with other forms of quantitative research, content analysis can describe phenomena and identify trends but we can usually only speculate about the reasons why. A final criticism is the tendency to focus on what is measurable rather than what is theoretically significant. This is captured by a quotation that Einstein is reputed to have kept on his office wall:

> Not everything that can be counted counts, and not everything that counts can be counted.

Stage 2 Deciding which documents to analyse and what to include in your sample

You have been introduced to the concept of sampling (Chapter 1) and to approaches in both qualitative research (Chapter 3) and quantitative research (Chapter 5). Applying this to documentary analysis, you need to develop clear rules about what should be included in the sample, known as inclusion criteria. These criteria identify what is a suitable document and excludes documents that fall outside your study.

ACTIVITY 6.2

In the case study, Sarah is interested in how newspapers have portrayed women with a diagnosis of schizophrenia. What inclusion criteria should Sarah use for her study?

Comment

In the case study, the inclusion criteria would be that the articles are news articles, rather than other forms of articles such as features. The articles must relate to an individual diagnosed with schizophrenia, which must be used in a clinical sense, not a colloquial or metaphorical sense, e.g. not 'his performance on the football pitch was schizophrenic'. Sarah has decided that she will use only articles from the latest full year.

One of the most common questions is what an acceptable sample size is. Documentary analysis is one of the research methods that has the greatest variability in sample size because the documents themselves are so variable. If you are studying government policy documents or inquiry reports that can be several hundred pages long, you will have a different sample size to someone analysing short newspaper articles. Consequently, this is an issue that is best discussed with your supervisor or equivalent.

What if I have too many or too few documents?

Once you have established an appropriate sample size for your study, a common difficulty is having too many or too few documents to choose from. To some extent, this can be controlled through your inclusion criteria, either by narrowing your criteria to reduce the number of documents or by widening your criteria to increase the number of documents that you include in your sample. In the case study, Sarah could reduce or increase the number of documents by looking for a shorter or longer time period or she could change other criteria such as including feature articles as well as news items.

However, you need to be careful not to distort your sample by using this approach. For example, Sarah could pick a short time period and this could coincide with a major news story about a person diagnosed with schizophrenia which would present a significantly different picture to another time period. A commonly used alternative approach when you have too many documents is to use random sampling, which is particularly appropriate for content analysis. Random sampling involves making a selection of cases (the sample) from the whole group of possible cases (the population) on the basis of chance. In random sampling, each case has an equal chance of being selected.

In Sarah's case, she completed an electronic search and found that there were 600 news articles involving people diagnosed with schizophrenia during 2008. Since this is too large a number to analyse, she decided to randomly select a 10 per cent sample, namely 60 articles. She could do this through a random number table or through an online random number generator (such as www.randomizer.org). Having obtained 60 random numbers between 1 and 600, she would select the articles from her search that corresponded to these numbers.

If you have too few documents, you need to consider whether a more qualitative analysis may be appropriate, depending upon your research question. In Chapter 7, qualitative approaches to data analysis such as thematic analysis will be outlined and these may be more appropriate.

Wherever possible, try to include documents in electronic format because the process of analysis is considerably easier. For example, if you are analysing government documents, try to download them from the relevant website in electronic format so that you can search for relevant terms using the search facility. If you are using newspaper articles, try to use electronic databases such as ProQuest (see the case study below). Consulting your library can be invaluable in identifying electronic resources for your research.

CASE STUDY

Sarah decided to use ProQuest, a national electronic database of newspaper articles from a range of national tabloid and broadsheet newspapers. The ProQuest database includes the Daily Mail, Daily Telegraph, Guardian, Times *and* Independent *newspapers. This was available through her university library and enabled her to undertake a preliminary search to establish how much material is available.*

In order to undertake her preliminary search, she must decide which search terms to use. Since she is searching for articles that refer to individuals diagnosed with schizophrenia, she used the search term 'schizo*'. The Boolean operator '*' is a wildcard, which means that all phrases that include the word stem 'schizo', e.g. schizophrenia, schizophrenic, will be included (see Chapter 2 for a detailed explanation of how to conduct a literature search).

She found that there are approximately 50 articles per month that refer to individuals diagnosed with schizophrenia, spread evenly over the year. Looking at a one-year time period, the search returned 600 articles spread evenly throughout the year. Sarah randomly chose a 10 per cent sample (60 articles) over the year. These took two days to code, working on the basis of approximately 10–15 minutes per article. Once Sarah had identified a suitable article, she was able to store it ready for analysis, making sure that she kept details of the source and date of the article.

Stage 3 Collecting and analysing your data

Firstly, you need to decide your basic unit of analysis, i.e. the amount of text you will be using for coding, such as a single word, phrase, sentence or a whole article (Neuman, 2006). In our case study, Sarah has decided to use a whole newspaper article as her research unit.

Secondly, you need to design a codebook and a recording sheet. A codebook is a set of instructions for coders that explains how documents are going to be coded. This includes guidance as to what is included under each dimension and what coders should take into account when deciding how to allocate a particular code. The aim of the codebook is to ensure that all documents are coded consistently and in a way that can be replicated by others.

In the case study, Sarah's codebook would look like Figure 6.1.

Codebook

Case Id – case identification number for article, numbered sequentially.

Gender of person with a diagnosis of schizophrenia in the news story

Please insert one of the following codes:

1 = female

2 = male

0 = not specified

Tabloid or broadsheet newspaper

Please insert one of the following codes:

1 = broadsheet

2 = tabloid

Publication Name of publication

Glasgow category i.e. categories developed by the Glasgow Media Group (1996)

1 = Violence to others

2 = Harm to self

3 = Prescriptive/advice

4 = Criticism of accepted definitions of mental illness

5 = 'Comic' images

6 = Other

Stigmatising language

0 = no stigmatising language

1 = stigmatising language

Prominence

1 = front page

2 = pages 2 or 3

3 = other page

Figure 6.1 Codebook

When coding your data, it is generally accepted (Sarantakos, 2005; Neuman, 2006) that there are four dimensions to consider: frequency, direction, prominence and intensity. Not all of the dimensions may be relevant and researchers may measure from one of these to all four dimensions (Neuman, 2006).

- *Frequency* Was the required unit of research present? For the case study, this would mean deciding whether schizophrenia was mentioned in the news article.

- *Direction* Was it positive, negative or neutral? This involves rating the content of the message along a scale. For the case study, this would mean whether the article presented the person diagnosed with schizophrenia in a positive, negative or neutral way.

- *Prominence* What prominence was given in the document? For Sarah's project, was the news story the front-page headline or was it on page 14?

- *Intensity* How powerful was the message? This measures the extent to which the unit of research is stressed. For Sarah, this would be the extent to which the person's mental health problem was stressed in the article.

The next stage is to design a recording sheet in order to document the results of your coding. Once you have designed your coding manual, you will start your analysis by taking your first document and begin coding it, i.e. identifying and classifying the aspects of the document that you have identified and writing this down on your recording sheet. In the case study, Sarah's recording sheet would look like Figure 6.2.

Case Id	Gender	Tabloid or broadsheet	Publication	Glasgow category	Stigmatising language	Prominence
1	2	1	Times	1	1	1
2	1	2	Mail	2	0	3
3	2	2	Mail	1	1	2
4	2	1	Independent	1	1	1
5	1	1	Guardian	4	1	1
6	2	2	Mail	1	1	1

Figure 6.2 Recording sheet

Developing your coding schedule in a spreadsheet package such as Excel is a useful way of recording and analysing data and can be exported into statistical software packages such as SPSS. Quantitative data are normally presented in the form of tables and graphs, which are discussed in detail in Chapter 8.

Advantages and disadvantages of documentary analysis

Documentary analysis has a number of advantages and disadvantages as a research method. One of the main advantages is that the data already exists so it is a matter of gaining access rather than gathering data yourself. It is an attractive research method because it avoids the time-consuming process of negotiating access to participants and arranging interviews or focus groups. This makes it economical to collect data, in terms of both cost and time. This is particularly true if you are using documents in electronic form because you will be able to organise text more easily and use search engines to enable you to locate items of interest. Since the documents already exist independently of your research, they cannot be biased by the researcher in the same way as interviews and focus groups.

As with all research designs, consideration needs to be given to ethical concerns and documentary analysis should not be considered an ethically neutral process (McCulloch, 2004). However, it presents lower ethical risks than other methods because it does not directly involve participants. Consequently ethical approval is often not required if you are using publicly available data. The highest risks relate to the use of sensitive information, such as client information, but issues around copyright, freedom of information and data protection need to be addressed by all research projects.

The availability of data means that it is easy to become overwhelmed by the amount of information and to find it difficult to decide what to leave out. Since you are analysing data outside the original context in which the document was produced, the framework that was used to create the original document may be significantly different to the framework you would use to analyse it. While this may produce valuable insights, it can be challenging.

Your research is limited by the documents that are available, both in scope and in quality. Since the documents that you study will have been produced for a different purpose than your research study, they are unlikely to focus solely on the issue you are interested in. The quality of the documents may be variable and if they are in different formats, they may be difficult to compare and may require considerable preparation before they can be analysed. For example, if you were comparing an inquiry report from the 1970s with a modern inquiry report, the quality, detail and format of the documents are likely to be quite different (Parton, 2004). There may be omissions and inaccuracies in the original documents and some documents may be more likely to survive than others. Although you cannot introduce bias into what is contained within the documents, your biases may influence the types of records you use and how you interpret them. These issues do not preclude using documentary analysis but would require discussing in your dissertation.

C H A P T E R   S U M M A R Y

This chapter has aimed to give you a clear outline of how to use documentary analysis as a research method for your project. Although it is one of the lesser known and used social research methods, it is likely to become more popular with the increase in the availability of documents in an electronic format. It is commonly confused with a literature review because they both involve analysing documents but it is important to understand the distinction. A framework for assessing the documents you choose to study has been discussed, using the four criteria of authenticity, credibility, representativeness and meaning. Content analysis has been discussed as a straightforward means of analysing data by converting them into a quantifiable form, but the limitations of this approach have also been discussed.

Atkinson, P and Coffey, A (1997) Analysing documentary realities. In D. Silverman (ed), *Qualitative research: Theory, method and practice*. London: Sage.
Interesting and useful discussion about documentary analysis from a qualitative perspective.

Bryman, A (2008) *Social research methods*, 3rd edition. Oxford: Oxford University Press.
Good discussion of content analysis and an excellent all-round research textbook.

Neuman, WL (2006) *Basics of social research: Qualitative and quantitative approaches, international*. 2nd edition. Boston, MA: Allyn & Bacon.
Detailed discussion of context analysis and a comprehensive general textbook.

Prior, L (2003) *Using documents in social research*. London: Sage.
Detailed account of documentary analysis from a qualitative perspective. Interesting discussion of philosophical basis for documentary analysis.

Scott, J (1990) *A matter of record: Documentary sources in social research*. Cambridge: Polity Press.
A classic text in documentary analysis, concentrating mainly on historical documents.

ProQuest (www.proquest.com)
A national electronic database of newspaper articles from a range of national tabloid and broadsheet newspapers. Normally available through your university library webpage.

Chapter 7
Analysing your data

Introduction

Data analysis is the process of making sense of the information you have collected and searching for what lies below the surface content. While the previous chapters have focused on how you will design your research project and obtain your data, this chapter will help you grasp how to understand the often complex story that your data tell.

Data analysis involves skills that we use every day in our social work practice. When we meet a new service user, we seek to understand their unique situation. When we have met a number of service users in similar situations, we start to see patterns in what they tell us. We try to identify similarities and differences and start to see links and relationships between the different aspects of their experiences. This helps us to build up our understanding of those experiences that can be helpful for new service users that we meet.

Data analysis also involves new skills and techniques which can seem daunting and confusing at first. If you see data analysis as being a highly technical, almost mystical process then it can be difficult to start. Conversely, if you feel that, once you have gathered your data, the findings will be obvious and writing up will be a straightforward task, then you can quickly become overwhelmed by the data and find it difficult to make sense of it all without some form of framework. This chapter aims to provide a clear and accessible guide that will take you through the process.

This chapter is divided into analysing qualitative and quantitative data. In the first part, we shall begin by examining a robust and straightforward approach to qualitative data analysis, thematic analysis (Braun and Clarke, 2006). This provides a clear framework for novice researchers and a six-stage model will be outlined.

In the second part on quantitative data analysis, you will be introduced to descriptive statistics as a useful framework for analysing your data from questionnaires or documentary analysis. Different levels of quantitative measurement will be outlined and guidance will be provided on appropriate forms of statistical analysis for each level. As you will remember from Chapter 1, data is a plural rather than a singular noun (the singular is 'datum').

Analysing qualitative data

The term 'data analysis' may conjure up images of number crunching and statistical tests. However, in qualitative research, the data you are analysing are words. These can be the words of your participants during interviews and focus groups or in texts if you are undertaking a documentary analysis. It is possible to analyse visual material or observational data, but these are specialised areas not covered in this book. In qualitative research, data analysis is the fascinating process of making sense of what people have said, identifying patterns and understanding meanings. Miles and Huberman (1994) capture the inherently interesting nature of this process:

> *Qualitative data are sexy. They are a source of well-grounded, rich descriptions and explanations of processes in identifiable local contexts. With qualitative data one can preserve chronological flow, see precisely which events led to which consequences, and derive fruitful explanations.*

(Miles and Huberman, 1994, p1)

In many respects, analysing your data has similarities with social work practice. In both roles, you are faced with rich and complex accounts and your task is to make sense of them. This involves seeing patterns and meaning in the accounts and it is inevitable that this involves you exercising your judgement. Just as there is no way of working with a service user that rigidly follows rules without considering context, the same is true of analysing your data.

Given the complexity of human communication, having hard and fast rules for making sense of meaning is unlikely to be helpful. Qualitative data analysis is a contested area, with no universally agreed rules. While there are broad guidelines to guide you, applying them requires you to exercise your judgement and make explicit decisions. This section will concentrate upon data collected from interviews and focus groups but the processes are equally applicable to documentary analysis using texts in a similar way to transcripts.

Before we look at how to analyse your data, it is necessary to discuss the process of writing up your transcripts and how to store your data ethically.

Writing up and storing your data ethically

Typing up your data

An important issue that you need to consider is how to write up your interviews or focus groups. This can range from detailed transcripts that record every word, pause and non-verbal communication to notes that capture the key features. Most people choose something in between these two extremes which is partly determined by what is expected by your university, so check this out with your supervisor. Highly detailed transcripts using specific transcription systems such as the Jefferson system (Atkinson and Heritage, 1984) are required for data analysis approaches such as conversational analysis but thematic analysis requires a more straightforward verbatim account (Braun and Clarke, 2006). Typing up your data enables you to move the text around and to copy and paste it into different files.

Formatting your transcripts

Transcripts should have double line spacing and include a separate column or wide margin for adding coding and other notes. It can be helpful to include line numbering on your transcripts. In Microsoft Word 2003, line numbering can be turned on by selecting 'file' then 'page setup', choosing the 'layout' tab and then clicking the 'line numbers' box. In Microsoft Word 2007, simply select 'page layout' then 'line numbers'. Leave sufficient time for transcription as it can be time-consuming, e.g. allow 2–6 hours to write up a one-hour interview, more for a focus group. Boyatzis (1998) states that the transcript from a one-hour interview can be 20–40 pages.

Password protecting or encrypting your transcripts

Once you have typed up your transcript, it is best ethical practice to password protect the file so that, in the event that it is lost, other people would not be able to open it. In Microsoft Word 2003, this is done by selecting the 'tools' menu, choosing 'options', then selecting the 'security' tab. You will be prompted to select a password that will be required by anyone wishing to open the file. In Microsoft Word 2007, you can encrypt the document by clicking on the main office button, selecting 'prepare' then 'encrypt document'.

Separate transcripts from participants' personal information

Another example of best ethical practice is to store the personal details of your participants in a separate place to the transcripts. The personal details form and the interview transcript are linked by a key in which each participant is given a number. This number is recorded on the transcript and the two sets of documents are kept separately so that if another party should gain unauthorised access to the transcripts, they will not be able to see the participant's identity or details.

Develop a short questionnaire for participants' personal information

A similar issue is that you may wish to ask participants some simple factual questions, e.g. age, ethnicity and length of experience. Since this information can make a participant highly identifiable in a transcript, it is usually wiser to develop a short questionnaire that participants can fill out and which can be stored separately from the transcript.

Think about your system of transcription

Decide what level of detail is required for your transcript. Do you need to include pauses, laughter, non-verbal communication? For thematic analysis, a good verbatim transcript is required but not in the same detail as, for example, conversation analysis. For a good account of transcription conventions, see Atkinson and Heritage (1984) or Silverman (2001, p303). It can be helpful on your transcripts to include background information about the interview to provide a context that may help you to understand the data. This will include where and when it took place and any factors that may be relevant, e.g. if the participant was tired, distracted, found the interview difficult. Do you transcribe silences and non-verbal communication? This can be very helpful, but it depends upon your research question and design.

Keep originals separate from your analysis copies

It is vital that you keep at least one electronic copy of your original transcript stored in a safe place. This is because there are few things more disheartening in research than working on a manuscript, coding it and moving text around, to discover that you have been working on your only copy of the original transcript. If you cannot reconstruct the original transcript, this could even necessitate re-transcribing the whole interview or focus group again.

Using thematic analysis

The model for analysing qualitative data in this book is thematic analysis, which is one of the most commonly used methods for analysing such data (Bryman, 2008; Davies, 2007). In this chapter, you will be introduced to a clear and systematic way of analysing your data based upon a model of thematic analysis developed by Braun and Clarke (2006).

Thematic analysis has been defined as *a method for identifying, analysing and reporting patterns (themes) within data* (Braun and Clarke, 2006, p79). It is a foundational method that teaches students core skills that are useful for other forms of qualitative analysis. Thematic analysis is a flexible approach that is compatible with different epistemological approaches. We have previously discussed the distinction between positivist/realist and interpretivist/social constructionist approaches (see Chapter 1 for a detailed discussion) and thematic analysis can be used with both approaches.

The process of thematic analysis

Braun and Clarke (2006) outline a six-stage model to guide you through the process of analysing your data. Before we look at this in detail, it is important to define some key terms. *Data set* refers to the total data that you will use in your analysis. *Data item* refers to a particular interview or focus group, while *data extract* refers to a passage that has been taken from a data item, e.g. a quote from an interview.

Phase 1: Becoming familiar with your data

The first stage of your analysis is to immerse yourself in your data by reading all of your transcripts at least once. This enables you to sensitise yourself to the material in all of your transcripts, i.e. the whole data set. As you collected and transcribed the data yourself, you will already have prior knowledge but seeing it written down can enable you to see new patterns. Although this can be time-consuming and it can be tempting to skip this, it will be time well spent. Read actively, searching for patterns in what you read and in making notes.

Phase 2: Creating initial codes

When you have familiarised yourself with your data, the next step is to generate your initial codes. A code is the most basic building block of the raw data and identifies a feature of the data that is of interest to the researcher (Braun and Clarke, 2006: Boyatzis, 1998). It may be helpful to look at an example to illustrate this process.

CASE STUDY

Emmanuel is a social work student on placement in a children's team. He is interested in how high-profile child deaths affect social workers working in children's services and has interviewed a number of front-line social workers. Having reread his interview transcripts thoroughly, Emmanuel started coding his first transcript and began with the passage from a childcare social worker shown in Figure 7.1.

Transcript	Codes
Interviewer: *How does a high-profile child death affect you as a social worker in children's services?*	
Participant 1: *It creates a lot more anxiety in front-line social workers, definitely. And it's hard to deal with that anxiety when you get so little supervision. So you tend to find ways to cope with it, some positive and some negative. The positive ways are that I tend to go out and visit children more, talk to them. And make sure I've got my paperwork up to date. The negative ways are that making sure all your home visits AND all your paperwork are up to date means I work even longer hours and get more tired so it's more likely I'll make a mistake.*	More anxiety Little supervision Positive ways of coping Negative ways of coping

Figure 7.1 Interview transcript

Comment

As you can see, the transcript is divided into two columns. In the first column are the words of the participants while the second column is left blank for your codes. The transcript should be double line spaced and it can be helpful to number the lines for ease of reference.

Your words or the participant's words?

One of the issues you must decide is whether you will use the participant's words when coding or your own words. In this example, the student has decided to use the participant's own words. Technically, this is known as *emic* or 'in vivo' coding because it relates to the words and phrases used by your participants. The alternative approach is *etic* or analytical codes, which are devised by the researcher and usually relate to the theoretical perspective that underpins the analysis. For example, if the same data were analysed using a psychoanalytic framework, the coding for 'ways of coping' might be termed 'defence mechanisms'.

The process of coding your data involves breaking it down into its smallest parts (codes) before rebuilding it into major patterns (themes). To use a metaphor, imagine your transcript as being made up of children's coloured bricks. When you are coding your data, you are breaking down what your participant said into its smallest constituent parts (bricks) and deciding what colour each part should be. For example, if your participant talked about 'negative ways of coping' during the interview, each example of this can be coded and given a particular colour, e.g. red. All of the 'red bricks' (data extracts coded as red) within the interview and across all of the interviews can then be gathered together.

The metaphor has its limitations because it suggests that the coloured building bricks are already contained in the data, while the complex reality is that you are required to identify and colour the bricks yourself. It may be tempting to think of data analysis as being a passive process of themes 'emerging' from your interview or focus group transcripts. At one level, this can be a reassuring image. It is comforting because it presents the view that knowledge exists out there to be discovered and implies that data analysis is an objective, scientific process in which the analyst has a passive, objective role. This is rarely a sustainable view once you have become actively involved in analysing your data, because you realise that it is an active process in which you must make choices and to which you bring your previous experiences. You may regard these as 'contaminants' or 'biases' that should be removed in order to obtain an 'objective' view. Within qualitative research, removing your own self and experiences from the research process is neither possible nor desirable. Instead, it is about being reflexive – about questioning your own assumptions and views and being open about these in your analysis.

As you code your data, it is important to give equal attention to all of your data, rather than focusing on those parts that may initially attract your attention. Material that may seem unpromising initially may become important later. Code for as many potential themes as possible and retain some of the surrounding data because this helps you to understand the context. Braun and Clarke (2006) state that some sections of your transcript may not be coded, while other sections may receive more than one code.

> *You can code individual extracts in as many different 'themes' as they fit into*
> *– so an extract may be uncoded, coded once, or coded many times, as*
> *relevant.*

> (Braun and Clarke, 2006, p89)

Once you have gathered together all the data extracts that relate to a particular code, open a new word processing file under that name. For example, if a code from the case study above is 'negative ways of coping', then create a new file using that name. Cut and paste the original data extracts from your first interview into the new file. As Emmanuel undertakes further interviews, he will add any further mention of 'negative ways of coping'. At the end of the process, he will have a file called 'negative ways of coping' that will contain all of the participants' words when they were discussing this topic (see Figure 7.2).

While this may seem time-consuming, it will save you time reviewing different transcripts and holding each data extract in your mind while you search for the next data extract. Once you have collected all the extracts together in one file, check whether they form a coherent pattern. If so, you can move on to the next stage. If the data extract does not fit, you have three choices: you could move it to another theme that is more appropriate, create a new theme or remove it from the analysis (Braun and Clarke, 2006).

By the end of this stage, you will have a large number of codes along with their related data extracts. In the next stage, you will be identifying themes, which means seeing which of the colours seem to link together, e.g. red bricks with pink and orange bricks. These wider groupings are your themes and you are likely to have a smaller number of them.

Code: *'Negative ways of coping'*

Participant 1
The negative ways are that making sure all your home visits AND all your paperwork are up to date means I work even longer hours and get more tired so it's more likely I'll make a mistake.
Participant 2
I find that a high-profile child death can have a negative effect because I tend to cope with it by going to my manager all the time for every minor decision because I feel less anxious if I share the responsibility.
Participant 3
I find that, after a high-profile child death, I document everything very carefully and defensively. Rather than writing your notes and thinking 'how would this look if the service user read it?', you start thinking 'how would this look if it was read out at any inquiry panel?' (Pause) It's quite frightening really, I try not to think about it

Figure 7.2 Coded extracts

Phase 3: Searching for themes

When you have coded all of your data and produced a list of the codes, the next phase is to group your codes into potential themes. In this phase, your aim is see how the codes can be grouped together into broader themes and how these themes relate to each other. Using the analogy of the coloured bricks, you have already broken down your transcript into their constituent bricks. In this phase, you are grouping the bricks into groups of similar or compatible colours, e.g. red bricks being grouped with pink and orange bricks.

A useful technique is to write your codes on sticky notes. You can put these onto a table, wall or floor and stand back to view them all. You may notice that some codes seem to belong together, so you can move the sticky notes around to group them together. In order to ensure you have an accurate understanding of each code, you will need to refer back to your transcript to clarify exactly what participants said

So what are themes? Themes are broader than codes and represent a higher level of abstraction. A theme *captures something important about the data in relation to the research question, and represents some level of patterned response or meaning within the data set* (Braun and Clarke, 2006, p82). There are no rigid rules because we are dealing with the complexities of meaning, so you will need to use judgement. However, you must do this transparently and consistently. While the frequency with which a topic arises in the transcript is likely to be significant, there are no hard and fast rules.

You need to think about whether the themes themselves are main or sub-themes. For example, Emmanuel has a theme of 'ways of coping', which has two sub-themes, negative and positive ways of coping. You also need to consider whether the themes have a relationship with each other, e.g. whether the themes of 'ways of coping' and 'lack of supervision' are linked with the theme of 'increased anxiety of practitioners'.

As your analysis progresses, you may find that some themes become more important while others become peripheral. Themes become more important because they say something significant about the research question or topic. You may find that some codes do not fit into any group and you can use a theme called 'miscellaneous' to group them under, possibly on a temporary basis (Braun and Clarke, 2006). Try not to abandon anything yet, because it is too early to determine whether particular themes will eventually be changed or discarded.

At the end of this phase, you will have developed a number of initial or candidate themes and sub-themes that you can organise into an initial thematic map (see Figure 7.3).

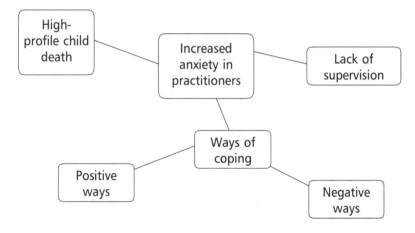

Figure 7.3 Thematic map

Phase 4: Reviewing themes

Having drawn up a list of potential or candidate themes and developed an initial thematic map, this phase focuses on reviewing and refining these themes. Data analysis, like so much of the research process, involves going back and forth between different stages in a recursive process.

In this phase, you are reviewing your themes at two levels. The first level is within the theme, in which you read all of the extracts from your transcripts coded within that theme. As you examine the data extracts for each theme, you will be evaluating critically whether the theme has sufficient data and whether they are sufficiently similar. You may find that some themes have insufficient data or the data are too dissimilar to sustain it as a theme. You may also find that what initially appears to be one theme needs to be split into two when you inspect the data more carefully. Alternatively, you may find that two initial themes eventually prove to form one larger theme.

Within each theme, the data should clearly relate to it and be distinct themes: *Data within themes should cohere together meaningfully, whilst th be clear and identifiable distinctions between themes* (Braun and Clarke, 20

Having reviewed within all of your themes, the second level is to review across your transcripts. You are reviewing the themes overall to check that they reflect the meanings apparent in the 'total data set'. You are standing back from the detailed reading of extracts to check whether the themes accurately reflect what participants said overall.

Phase 5: Defining and naming themes

Having developed a suitable thematic map, your task is to define and refine your themes. Work to identify names that capture the core of what the theme is about – this requires you to review the data extracts upon which it was based. Rather than just paraphrasing the verbatim content, identify the key features that are of interest. Within some themes, you may be able to identify sub-themes that organise the material and which need to be named.

By the end of this stage, you will have a clear idea about what is included and what is not included in each theme. You will have achieved this when you are able to describe each theme in a couple of sentences and have identified names that are succinct while conveying a clear sense of what the theme is about. Each theme should receive a detailed analysis, including how it fits into the overall narrative about your data.

Phase 6: Producing the report

This stage begins when you have decided on your final set of themes and thematic map. Your final report should be a coherent, convincing and interesting account of the story your data tell. This stage will be discussed in detail in Chapter 8, which focuses on writing up your research project.

Using qualitative data analysis (QDA) software

So far it has been assumed that you will be coding your data manually, but qualitative data analysis (QDA) software is another alternative. Packages such as NVivo8, AtlasTi, MaxQDA and the Ethnograph can separate out data extracts according to the code you have assigned them and help you map out how they relate to each other. However, it can be expensive if your university does not have a site licence and it can be time-consuming to learn how to use the software. Above all, the software does not do the analysis for you; it simply makes your own analysis easier once you have learnt how to use it. See Gibbs (2007) for a recent discussion of different software packages.

Analysing quantitative data

The focus of this section is to provide you with a toolkit of analytic procedures based upon descriptive statistics which will enable you to summarise patterns in your quantitative data. We will not cover more advanced inferential statistics because, although they are valuable, they require a significant amount of time and investment that is usually not practicable given the other demands of the social work degree.

The case study uses questionnaires, but the principles remain the same for other forms of quantitative data, such as using content analysis to analyse documents (see Chapter 6).

There are three stages of data analysis:

1. Coding your data.
2. Entering and cleaning your data.
3. Analysing your data and presenting your findings.

The first stage of data analysis is coding your data. You will have already pre-coded your data as part of developing your questionnaire (Chapter 5) or documentary analysis (Chapter 6). Using the example of a questionnaire, you will have already decided how you will code particular responses to questions. Let us look at an example to follow the process which you were introduced to in Chapter 5.

> **CASE STUDY**
>
> *Varsha is interested in using questionnaires to study her fellow students' attitudes towards their professional training. She wants to know whether final-year students feel that their training course had prepared them for the realities of working as qualified professionals. Figure 7.4 is a short extract from her questionnaire which has been pre-coded.*

Comment

The code underneath each response denotes what code to enter when the questionnaires are completed. For example, a 32-year-old female participant who agrees that her social work degree has developed her self-confidence would be coded as:

Q.1 1
Q.2 32
Q.3 2

The second stage of the process is entering your data onto a spreadsheet and cleaning it. Cleaning data is the process of checking that data have been entered accurately and are not missing or inaccurate. In this example, a spreadsheet is used but it is also possible to use a database package such as Microsoft Access (see Schneider et al., 2005) or a statistical package such as SPSS.

1. Are you female or male?

    Please tick ✓ one box only

    Female   Male

    ☐   ☐

    1   2

2. What was your age at your last birthday?

    Please write in box   ☐

3. To what extent do you agree or disagree that your professional social work degree has helped you to develop your self-confidence?
    Please tick ✓ one box only

	Strongly agree	Agree	Neither agree nor disagree	Disagree	Strongly disagree
	☐	☐	☐	☐	☐
Code	5	4	3	2	1

Figure 7.4 Extract from questionnaire

Questionnaire 1	Q.1 Gender	Q.2 Age	Q.3 Self-confidence
1	1	23	1
2	1	32	3
3	2	40	2
4	1	19	3
5	1	24	2
6	2	29	2
7	1	31	4
8	2	35	2
9	1	44	5
10	2	54	1

Figure 7.5 Excel spreadsheet

Each questionnaire is numbered sequentially and it is helpful to write this number on the front of the questionnaire for future referencing and checking. Once your data have been entered, it is necessary to clean your data by checking for missing or inaccurate data. Check that there are the correct number of questionnaires entered and that the codes entered are plausible, e.g. the first question about gender has either a '1' or '2' coding, so an entry of 32 is likely to be inaccurate. If there are blank spaces on the spreadsheet, go back to the questionnaire to check that the response is actually missing from the questionnaire itself. Once this has been completed, recheck all of your questionnaires against the data entered or, if there are a large number of them, check a sample for accuracy.

What should I do about missing data?

Missing data arises when respondents fail to respond to a question, either by accident or because they do not want to. There are a number of ways of dealing with missing data (Hertel, 1976; De Vaus, 2002):

- **Delete cases**   If there is a small number of cases (usually under 15 per cent) that account for the missing variables, these questionnaires can be deleted. Questionnaires that have significant amounts of missing data may be suspect in their data quality anyway, but losing a significant number may present problems for your analysis.

- **Delete variables**   If there is a particular question that accounts for a large number of missing data, this could be deleted. This would mean that you would not lose any cases, but it depends upon how important the question is for your overall analysis.

- **Sample mean approach**   Another approach is to replace the missing value with the mean of the other responses.

The third stage is analysing your data. You will be using descriptive statistics to make sense of your data and there are a number of measures/procedures that you can use. However, not all of the measures/procedures can be used on all types of quantitative data so it is necessary to understand the different levels of measurement.

Different levels of measurement of quantitative data

In order to be able to analyse quantitative data, it is necessary to understand that there are different levels of measurement that lead to different types of data. Although this may initially appear a little technical, it is necessary to understand these different types of data because they are treated differently. The different levels of measurement are as follows:

- **Nominal**   data placed into named categories, such as male/female, which do not have a particular order. Although numbers may be used to code nominal data, these do not have arithmetical qualities. These are the most basic form of data and are not amenable to most forms of statistical analysis.

- **Ordinal**   data placed into categories that have an order, a relationship with each other, e.g. a Likert scale on a questionnaire in which the participant chooses 'strongly agree, agree, neutral, disagree, strongly disagree'. We can infer the rank order but not the relative size. For example, we can infer that a participant who ticks 'strongly agree' holds the opinion more intensely than one who ticks 'agree'. However, we cannot infer whether, for example, the first participant feels twice or three times as strongly as the second, only the rank order.

- **Interval**   like ordinal data but ranked on a scale with equal intervals between categories, e.g. temperature. The scale does not have a zero point anchored in the real world, e.g. Celsius has a zero point that is arbitrarily set at the temperature that water freezes, but 50°C is not twice as hot as 25°C. This enables a wider range of mathematical procedures to be used.

- **Ratio**   like interval data, but the categories have a scale with a true zero point, e.g. age, income. These are the most valued level of data because they enable a full range of mathematical procedures to be used.

Types of quantitative analysis

We can now look at the different types of descriptive statistics that are available to you when analysing and presenting your data.

Frequency tables and percentages

Frequency tables enable you to show the incidence of particular responses. Percentages enable you to show figures as a proportion of the whole and can make data easier to understand. These will be discussed in more detail in Chapter 8 on presenting your findings.

What is the average? Measures of central tendency

Measures of central tendency report a typical or average value. The three main measures of central tendency are the mean, the median and the mode.

The *mean* is the arithmetic average, calculated by adding up the value of all of the responses and dividing by the number of responses received. It can only be used with interval and ratio data which have true arithmetical properties. The *median* is the middle point, when data are lined up in order. If you have an even number of data, it is half-way between the two middle values. The median can be used with any type of numerical data. The *mode* is the most common response given and can be used with all four types of data.

Since different questions produce different types of data (nominal, ordinal, ratio and interval), you need to ensure that the measure of central tendency (mean, mode and median) is appropriate for the type of data you are collecting. Applying this to the case study, we can see that the questionnaire produces nominal, ordinal and ratio data, which should be treated differently.

ACTIVITY **7.1**

Look at the case study questionnaire and decide which questions produce nominal, ordinal and ratio data.

Comment

Nominal data

You can see that it is the first question on gender that produces *nominal* data because, although numerical codes are given (female = 1, male= 2), the data do not have arithmetical qualities. The mean cannot be used because it would be meaningless to calculate an 'average gender' of 1.5. Therefore only the mode and the median would be appropriate measures to use. In this example, there are six female and four male participants so the mode is 1(= female) and the median is 1(= female).

Ordinal data

The third question, which uses a Likert scale to measure whether participants agree or disagree that their professional social work helped them to develop self-confidence, produces *ordinal* data. Although the coding for the Likert scales above is numbered 1–5, it would be equally valid to use the letters A–E instead. Consequently, it is important that they are not treated as if they had real numerical qualities, e.g. trying to calculate a mean would be inappropriate and misleading. The data have a mode of 2 = agree because this is the most frequent response. If the responses are lined up in order of magnitude, the median is also 2 = agree (there are an even number of responses, but the two middle scores are both 2). Just as above, it would, however, be inappropriate to work out a mean score because they are ordinal data and therefore do not have full numerical qualities, i.e. the score 4 (= disagree) is not twice the size of the score 2(= agree).

Ratio data

The second question, which is about the participants' age, produces ratio data that have full numerical qualities, e.g. someone who is 40 years old is twice as old as someone who is 20 years old. Consequently, it would be appropriate to work out the mean by dividing the total sum of the responses with the number of respondents (= 331/10), which gives us a mean of 33.2 years. The mode and median are also appropriate measures. In this example, there is no mode because no response appears more than once. The median is 31.5 years because, once the responses are lined up in numerical order, the two middle responses are 31 and 32 years so they are averaged by being added together and divided by two.

Figure 7.6 summarises the appropriate descriptive statistics for different levels of measurement.

	Mode	Median	Mean
Nominal	✓	✗	✗
Ordinal	✓	✓	✗
Interval	✓	✓	✓
Ratio	✓	✓	✓

Figure 7.6 Appropriate descriptive statistics for different levels of measurement

What is the range? Measures of dispersion

Measures of dispersion indicate the degree of variety or spread of the data. Providing averages can be helpful for understanding the midpoint of data, but it is also important to look at the spread. The simplest way is using the range, which gives the lowest and highest points. Using this case study, the first ten participants had a mean age of 32.2 years, and the range was 19–54 years.

The final part of this third stage of your analysis is presenting and writing up your results. This will be discussed in depth in Chapter 8, where the use of tables and graphs for presenting quantitative data will be outlined.

Avoiding common mistakes in data analysis

The following are common mistakes that are made in both qualitative and quantitative data analysis, and also have parallels in social work practice:

- ***Don't overestimate first impressions***   Be aware that our initial thoughts can make a significant impression so that we tend to resist later revision (Robson, 2002).

- ***Don't under- or overreact to new information***   Similarly, we tend to either resist revision or overestimate the significance of later data (Robson, 2002).

- ***Follow up outliers, look for negative cases and check out rival explanations*** (Miles and Huberman, 1994)   Outliers are examples that do not follow the trend, whilst negative cases are those that directly contradict the pattern that you have established. Use both to think about rival explanations that may provide a better account of your data.

- ***Don't undervalue data that are missing or difficult to obtain***   Be aware that there is a natural tendency to undervalue data that are either missing or difficult to obtain. These data may be at least as important as the data that you were able to collect (Robson, 2002).

- ***Recognise that some data are stronger than others and some data sources are more reliable***   For example, this applies to data that you have obtained directly rather than collected by another person (Miles and Huberman, 1994).

C H A P T E R   S U M M A R Y

In this chapter, we have discussed the processes involved in analysing qualitative and quantitative data. You have been invited to consider how the skills involved in data analysis are often skills that you use in your social work practice. Thematic analysis has been presented as a clear and systematic model for analysing qualitative data using a six-stage approach. Analytical procedures based upon descriptive statistics have been outlined to enable you to summarise patterns in your quantitative data. What is common between both forms of analysis is that you need to be clear and consistent in how you analyse your data. Finally, some of the common mistakes that affect all forms of data analysis have been highlighted.

FURTHER READING

For qualitative data analysis

Braun, V and Clarke, V (2006) Using thematic analysis in psychology. *Qualitative Research in Psychology*, 3, pp77–101.
A comprehensive and well-written article that covers the theoretical and pragmatic issues around thematic analysis and presents a clear and detailed account of the process.

Miles, MB and Huberman, AM (1994) *Qualitative data analysis: An expanded sourcebook*. 2nd edition. London: Sage.
Classic and highly influential textbook that provides a good background to qualitative data analysis.

The Computer Assisted Qualitative Data Analysis Software (CAQDAS) Networking Project (http://caqdas.soc.surrey.ac.uk/) provides practical support, training and information in the use of a range of software programs designed to assist qualitative data analysis.

Quantitative data analysis

De Vaus, DA (2002) *Surveys in social research*. 5th edition. London: Routledge.
Classic text on surveys that provides a good overview of the process.

Sapsford, R (2007) *Survey research*, 2nd edition. London: Sage.
A readable and useful guide to survey research.

Chapter 8

Writing up your dissertation

A C H I E V I N G   A   S O C I A L   W O R K   D E G R E E

This chapter will help you to meet the following standards as set out by the Quality Assurance Agency (2008) Subject Benchmark Statement for the social work degree:

- The critical application of research knowledge from the social and human sciences, and from social work (and closely related domains) to inform understanding and to underpin action, reflection and evaluation (4.2).
- Acquire and apply the habits of critical reflection, self-evaluation and consultation, and make appropriate use of research in decision-making about practice and in the evaluation of outcomes (4.7).
- Research-based concepts and critical explanations from social work theory and other disciplines that contribute to the knowledge base of social work, including their distinctive epistemological status and application to practice (5.1.4).
- Knowledge and critical appraisal of relevant social research and evaluation methodologies, and the evidence base for social work (5.1.4).
- Use research critically and effectively to sustain and develop . . . practice (5.8).
- Demonstrate sufficient familiarity with statistical techniques to enable effective use of research in practice (5.9).
- An ability to use research and inquiry techniques with reflective awareness, to collect, analyse and interpret relevant information (7.3).

Introduction

This final chapter discusses how to write up your whole project. Having gathered and analysed your data, your final stage is producing your dissertation. This is likely to be the longest piece of independent work that you will submit for your course, so careful attention to structure and presentation is needed to ensure clarity and compliance with the university's requirements.

In this chapter, we will discuss the writing process itself and some of the barriers that can inhibit that process. You will be introduced to the structure of the traditional dissertation and how to present your findings in a clear and cogent way. The differences between presenting quantitative and qualitative research will be outlined. The terms 'dissertation', 'project' and 'study' are used as synonymous here to refer to the written report of your research. Usage by different courses varies so check with your university.

The process of writing

Writing up your research dissertation can be both exciting and daunting because it is unlike your previous coursework in two ways. Firstly, it has a structure and terminology that is unlike the standard essay format. Secondly, it is likely to be the longest piece of work that you complete on your course.

The writing process itself can be a source of anxiety. Becker describes running a seminar on writing skills and found that students identified two main fears:

> They were afraid that they would not be able to organise their thoughts, that writing would be a big confused chaos that would drive them mad. They spoke feelingly about a second fear, that what they wrote would be 'wrong' and that (unspecified) people would laugh at them.

(Becker, 2007, p4)

Becker (2007) found that students adopted a number of coping mechanisms to manage their anxiety, for example using particular pens or paper, sharpening pencils or cleaning the house (he found a gender divide on the latter!).

ACTIVITY 8.1

Can you relate to these fears? Are there different concerns and anxieties you have about writing?

Comment

You may have been able to see yourself in Becker's comments. Or there may be other anxieties and concerns that you were able to identify. The important point is to not let yourself be paralysed by your anxieties.

One common barrier is the belief that you must read everything that is written on your topic and work out your ideas before you put them down. The danger is that writing is continually postponed while you read and think some more. Start writing as soon as you can because the writing process helps us to identify your thoughts. Becker expresses it well when he states:

> Writing a dissertation starts with writing, not with preparing to write ... And feeling unready is no excuse at all. In scholarship, one is never ready, since there is always something else that one can sensibly read. All scholarship, strictly speaking, is at first written by the unprepared, or at least by the under-prepared ... Since you are never ready to write, you start writing before you are ready.

(Becker, 1986, p88).

Delamont, et al. (2004) offer two golden rules for writing your dissertation:

- *Write early and write often*   The more you write, the easier it gets and it becomes a habit. The later you leave it to start writing, the more difficult it can become. Work out the times that you are most productive and try to develop a routine of writing something everyday.

- *Don't get it right, get it written*   Drafting is an essential stage in working out what you want to say. In previous smaller essays on single topics, it may have been possible to hold everything in your head and work out everything that you want to say. You have simply too much material and often a series of related topics that you progressively develop, so drafting is an essential part of the process of working out what you want to say. As you write, you are likely to see some of the tensions, contradictions and inconsistencies in your argument (Delamont et al., 2004, p121).

Free writing, in which you write down whatever comes into your head without censoring or editing, can help you to establish what you want to say without being paralysed by choices (Becker, 2007). It helps you to realise that you can write your ideas down without fear and that the only draft that counts is the final draft.

ACTIVITY *8.2*

Write for 5–10 minutes about your thoughts and feelings concerning writing up your dissertation and what barriers you envisage. If you run out of things to say, repeat your last word continuously until further words come to you.

Comment

This is a useful exercise for two reasons. Firstly, you experience the process of free writing and how liberating and frightening it can be to write whatever comes into your head. It can be a powerful lesson in how we often do not know what we think about a subject until we see what we have written down on the page. Secondly, the content of what you have written helps you to understand the potential barriers to you completing your dissertation. These barriers can be physical, e.g. finding and protecting the time given the other demands of the course and your personal and work life. They can also be psychological, such as the fear that you will not be able to produce academic work of the required standard. This fear is particularly common and can partly explain why dissertations are often delayed more than other pieces of coursework (although other reasons, such as delays in getting ethical approval or access to participants are at least as important). Identifying these barriers will help you plan to overcome them.

Structuring your dissertation

Check whether your university provides you with specific guidelines for how to structure your research project. This is particularly true if your university has developed a structure that is specific to that course. However, most universities use a traditional dissertation format and provide less detailed guidance, so this chapter will be important for helping you know how to structure your work.

The traditional dissertation layout has the following format:

1. *Title page* Check your university's rules about the exact format.

2. *Table of contents* This provides a clear guide to where readers can find particular sections.

3. *Abstract* This provides a summary of your research, including a brief account of your research design and findings.

4. *Introduction* This should introduce your research question and explain why it is important. It should outline your approach and clarify the structure of the dissertation.

5. *Literature review* This is a coherent and critical account of the literature that provides an overall argument based upon your reading of the literature.

6. *Methodology* This explains in clear and specific terms how you conducted your research. It includes an overview of what you did, why you made your choices and how you addressed ethical issues.

7. *Findings and discussion* In quantitative dissertations, the presentation of findings is usually separated from the discussion section while they are combined for qualitative research.

8. *Conclusion* The conclusion should summarise your research and its major components together with the principal findings and how they relate to the literature. The conclusion could include recommendations for policy and practice and for future research, listing possible areas of inquiry.

9. *References* These should be presented in the appropriate format for your university.

10. *Appendices* These provide additional background information, such as your interview schedule or questionnaire and sample information sheets given to participants.

Writing your abstract

Although your abstract appears first, it is written last. Abstracts are commonly 250–350 words and the aim is to condense your research project into a short summary. Your abstract contains the basic message of your research and should include your research question or topic, methodology, findings and their significance for the field.

Look at the journal articles that you have read for your literature review. Each contains an abstract that is carefully crafted because the authors know that most readers will search the literature using bibliographic databases containing abstracts only. If the abstract is badly written and unclear, few readers will take the time to read the whole article. Use them as examples to inform your writing.

Writing your introduction

This should introduce your research question and explain why it is important. Stating that it is a long-standing interest for you is not enough on its own. You need to show how it is relevant to the field of social work.

As a general guide, your introduction should start with your main aims and provide a short summary of the background context of your study. You should be clear about the main problem or issues to be investigated and present your overall approach. Finally, you should provide a short description of the structure of your dissertation (Walliman, 2006).

You do not have to start writing by working on the introduction. Indeed, there is a good argument for writing your introduction last, because it is at that stage that you will have a good idea of what you are going to say. It is not uncommon to read dissertation introductions that state that a particular topic will be discussed, then find that the main body of the dissertation is about something different. This is usually because the writer has developed their thinking and discovered that their research is really about the second topic rather than the first. This is a healthy part of the research process, but you need to ensure that you redraft your introduction to reflect it.

Writing your literature review

In Chapter 2, you were introduced to different ways of structuring your literature review. A popular approach is the chronological structure, which begins with the early development of the field and progresses through to the most recent developments. For example, Patrick (Chapter 4) is interested in social workers' views on the barriers to fathers being involved in parenting assessments. His literature review would discuss previous writing on the involvement of fathers where there are child welfare concerns. A chronological structure would examine how the topic has been discussed during different time periods.

Alternatively, he could adopt a thematic approach that focused on particular issues identified in the literature, such as media representations of fatherhood or the growing awareness of domestic violence. This could have a funnel structure, looking at the wider context of social policy and public perceptions of fathers and progressively narrowing down to the involvement of fathers in parenting assessments. Either structure is acceptable and good dissertations will give a clear rationale for the structure selected.

Avoid phrases such as 'research tells us...' unless you are prepared to state exactly which research studies you are referring to and provide some form of critical analysis of them. Your marker is unlikely to let vague references to unspecified research go unchallenged at this stage in your studies.

Rather than taking things at face value, a good literature review will address the contradictions and omissions in previous writings. It will also address issues of power and demonstrate awareness that some viewpoints are subjugated while others are privileged.

Writing your methodology section

Journalists are taught that the first sentence of a newspaper article should answer the following questions: who, what, when, where, why and sometimes how (Leki, 1998, p25). While academic readers are likely to be more forgiving, these questions are useful to guide your methodology section. Your methodology section should usually address the following areas:

- *Overall research approach and methods* What was your overall approach (qualitative or quantitative)? What research methods did you use to collect your data (interviews, questionnaires, focus groups)? Why did you choose this approach and research method compared to alternative approaches?

- *Sampling* Who did you have as participants? What was the size and composition of your sample? How did you select and contact them? Where did you go to get access to them?

- *Analysis* How did you analyse your data? Why did you choose that particular approach?

- *Ethical issues* How did you address ethical issues, such as gaining access to participants or other sources of data, informed consent, confidentiality, anonymising data and ethical data management?

- *Limitations* What are the limitations of your research? This discussion can begin here and be developed further in the discussion of your findings.

Presenting and discussing your qualitative data

In qualitative dissertations, the presentation of findings is in prose form and lends itself to being discussed immediately. Consequently, findings and discussion are usually combined into one section.

In Chapter 7, thematic analysis was outlined as a good model for analysing most forms of qualitative data. The six-stage model developed by Braun and Clarke (2006) was outlined and the first five stages were described in detail. Our focus in this chapter is on the final stage, writing up and presenting your analysis.

The final stage begins when you have established and refined your themes. Your task in writing up your analysis is *to tell the complicated story of your data in a way which convinces the reader of the merit and validity of your analysis* (Braun and Clarke, 2006, p93). Your aim is to provide a concise and coherent narrative that contains sufficient quotes that demonstrate your themes without becoming repetitive. Do not present your quotes without explanation and expect the reader to make the connections themselves. Just as you would make an argument and provide a quote from a book or article as evidence to strengthen your argument, use the quotes from your participants in a similar way. Choose particularly vivid and concise quotes that demonstrate your point as closely as possible. Better to have one or perhaps two crisp quotes rather than include three or four more general quotes. Your quotes need to illustrate a narrative that presents an argument about how the data respond to your research question.

Your findings should be organised according to the themes identified in your analysis (see Chapter 7), rather than just using your interview or focus group questions as a structure. If you just summarise what participants said in response to questions 1, 2 and so on, this presents an impression that you have merely described your data rather than analysed it. Avoid using statistics to present your findings when you have small sample sizes. Stating '80 per cent of participants' sounds more dramatic than 'four out of five participants' but your reader is aware of your sample size and is unlikely to be convinced.

The key ethical issue in your findings section is protecting the confidentiality of your participants. The highest risk often occurs when you use a quote and identify a participant by a characteristic, such as their role, gender, ethnicity or sexual orientation. If the group that the participant belongs to is small, there is a high risk that other participants or other interested parties would be able to identify them. Consequently, avoid identifying a participant in this way – it rarely detracts significantly from your analysis. If you feel that you must, you may need to show your final draft to the participant to obtain their permission.

Presenting and discussing your quantitative data

In quantitative research, the presentation of findings is in table and graph form so it is conventional to split findings and discussion into two separate headings. A common practice is to include your raw data as an appendix at the back and draw upon the key data in the main body of your dissertation to illustrate your argument. Charts and tables should be in the body of the text, not as an appendix, otherwise it is difficult for the reader to follow your argument.

CASE STUDY

Varsha's quantitative research project
In Chapter 5, you met Varsha who is a final-year student interested in whether social work students felt that their training course was preparing them for the realities of working as qualified professionals. She used a questionnaire to study participants' levels of confidence overall and in specific areas of practice. She is considering how she will present her findings in her dissertation.

There is a range of tables and graphs that would be appropriate for Varsha to use to present her findings.

- *Frequency tables* present information about the relative occurrence of different values. They are useful when information is difficult to present in graph form because the highest and lowest values are significantly different or a high level of precision is required. An example is shown in Figure 8.1. Note that the *n* column indicates the actual number of responses. This lets the reader know how many responses were received and whether there were missing data.

	n	*per cent*
Strongly agree	6	12
Agree	24	48
Neither agree nor disagree	11	22
Disagree	6	12
Strongly disagree	3	6
Total	*50*	*100*

Figure 8.1 Frequency table: 'Overall, to what extent do you agree or disagree that your professional social work degree is preparing you for practice?'

- *Pie charts* enable you to present information about the relative proportions of different elements (see Figure 8.2) when the values are added together or you have only one set of data that all have positive values.

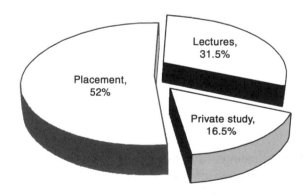

Figure 8.2 Pie chart: 'How important have the following parts of your training been to your professional development?'

- ***Bar graphs*** enable you to compare data across categories (see Figure 8.3). Simple bar graphs present single values and clustered bar graphs present groups of values together.

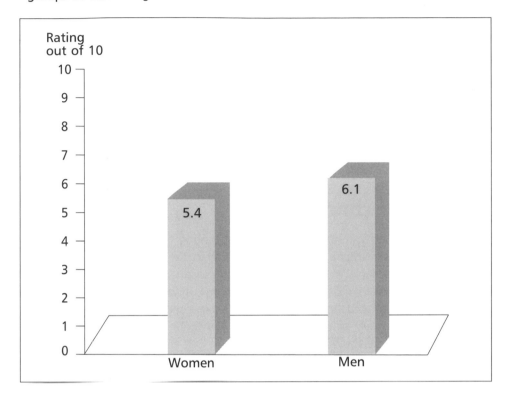

Figure 8.3 Bar chart: 'Overall, how would you rate how confident you feel about your ability to practise social work competently?'

Make your presentation of data attractive and clear. Always give a chart a title and make sure it is clear what it represents. Mark the axes to show scale and include legends to indicate actual figures or percentages. For a detailed discussion of the presentation of quantitative data, see Dunleavy (2003).

Although the general principles of presenting quantitative data are straightforward, it can take time to get it right in practice. Indeed, Delamont et al. (2004) argue that you should 'expect to suffer' about the presentation of statistics. Although this may be a little pessimistic, do allow yourself sufficient time.

In quantitative research, a separate discussion section enables you to examine the significance of your findings. This can be compared to other studies or to theories in your field. The discussion of your findings enables you to revisit your original research question and explore what you have learnt.

Avoid over-generalising your findings. What you may find in one setting in one area at one point in time can rarely be generalised to all populations at all points in time and it is important to be clear about this in your findings section. Silverman captures this eloquently:

> *It always helps to make limited claims about your own research. Grandiose claims about originality, scope or applicability to social problems are all hostages to fortune. Be careful in how you specify the claims of your approach. Show that you understand that it constitutes one way of 'slicing the cake' and that other approaches, using other forms of data, may not be directly competitive.*

(Silverman, 2005, p49)

In research, it is always wise to be realistic about what you can claim based upon your evidence and better to understate rather than overstate your findings.

Writing your conclusion

The conclusion should summarise your research and its major components together with the principal findings and how they relate to the literature. You should not introduce new material at this stage. Your conclusion could discuss lessons learnt from the process of research as well as the findings. It could also include recommendations for policy and practice in your research area and for future research, listing possible areas of inquiry or research designs. Try to be specific rather than simply stating that 'further research should be done'.

Some general points

Should I use 'I' in my dissertation?

Traditionally, students were encouraged to use the passive voice, e.g. 'the research interviews were conducted with six participants', rather than the active voice, e.g. 'I conducted interviews with six participants'. Students were particularly instructed to avoid using 'I' because it appeared too informal and not compatible with the 'scientific' tone expected. Within quantitative research using a positivist approach, this convention is usually still observed though the active voice is gradually becoming more acceptable. In qualitative research, the active voice is encouraged and 'I' is used more frequently, because reflexivity is actively encouraged.

Your choice should be guided by whether your research is quantitative or qualitative and by the expectations of your university and supervisor. If you do choose to use 'I', use it sparingly. Avoid overuse, e.g. 'I think that I found that I was approaching my topic because I feel I had previously viewed my beliefs...' Use 'I' when it genuinely adds something to what you are saying.

Structuring your dissertation

This is not just about headings. A good dissertation includes clear signposting. Since you are taking your reader on a journey, it is important to provide clear statements about where you are going and where you have been. At the end of each section, recap and tell the reader what you will be discussing next.

The function of sentences and paragraphs

A sentence is used to express a single idea. If a sentence expresses two or more ideas, you are probably making it work too hard. Try splitting it into two sentences for greater clarity. A paragraph consists of several sentences grouped together to express a set of related ideas. Consequently, one-sentence paragraphs are to be avoided.

Knowing what to leave out

Do not feel that you have to use every piece of material that you have gathered through the research process. The marker will want you to show you can construct an argument and use material selectively. This requires you to leave out material that is not relevant, which is much better than trying to 'shoehorn' extraneous material into your dissertation because you have expended considerable effort in obtaining it. A good researcher knows that the quality of research is as much about what is left out as what is included.

Referencing and proofreading your work

Referencing in your dissertation is no different to referencing an essay or any other piece of academic work. Most UK universities have adopted the Harvard referencing system and have produced help sheets to provide guidance. Check with your university website or library. Even if you know the Harvard system well, it is worthwhile checking because there are minor differences between universities about how they have interpreted the Harvard system. Many students feel that this is relatively unimportant, but good referencing does impress markers so it is well worth learning how to reference accurately.

One of the most common mistakes is for your references to omit texts that you have cited and to include texts that you have not. This is usually because you have included your references as you have worked on your drafts but not checked them at the end. So, as you have reworked your material, you have cut out material but left the original references in. Conversely, you have included material that cites texts that you have not yet put in your references. This mismatch between dissertation and references is surprisingly common, even with otherwise diligent students.

As you are writing, ensure that you save your work frequently and keep back-up copies. As a general rule, keep a back-up copy on one or more removable drives and e-mail yourself a copy regularly. This ensures that, even if your computer and removable drives were destroyed, you would still have a copy of your work.

Finally, careful proofreading is always worthwhile because it makes it easier for readers to understand what you are saying. Try to complete your dissertation a week before the deadline. This enables you to reread your dissertation with fresh eyes. Ideally, enlist another person because they are more likely to identify mistakes or confusions that you may miss.

If you have checked your spelling and grammar, markers are more likely to notice what you have to say rather than be distracted by poor presentation and typing mistakes. Coco Chanel reputedly said, 'Dress shabbily and they notice the clothes. Dress well and they notice the person.' The same is true of writing.

Disseminating and publishing your work

Completing your dissertation is a significant achievement. Having met the requirements of your degree, it may be tempting to just put it proudly on your bookshelf. However, it is worth considering how to disseminate your research to a wider audience. Managers, colleagues, service users and carers are all stakeholders that could benefit from hearing the results of your research. This can range from a presentation or short summary to writing for a professional or academic publication. If you are considering this, speak to your supervisor who may be able to provide useful help and advice. If you enjoyed your research project, you may also want to discuss opportunities for further research with them, either independently or as part of further study.

C H A P T E R   S U M M A R Y

In this chapter, the key messages are to start writing early and to use the writing process to help you work out what you want to say. Do not expect to be able to submit your first draft. You will usually need to draft material more than once before it is ready.

Adopt a clear structure to your dissertation and explain it in your introduction. Check with your supervisor and university in the early stages whether your structure is acceptable. In addition to your headings, you should guide the reader through it with clear 'signposting', i.e. explaining at each stage the stage that has been reached and what you are going to discuss next. Finally, try to get your dissertation ready before the deadline to allow time for a final proofreading as this will pay dividends.

FURTHER READING

Becker, H (2007) *Writing for social scientists: How to start and than finish your thesis, book or article*, 2nd edition. Chicago, IL: University of Chicago Press.
A classic text that provides a very readable and entertaining account of the writing process.

Conclusion

This book has attempted to provide a comprehensive guide to undertaking the research component of your social work degree. It has provided you with a framework for understanding the different stages, from developing a research question to writing up your findings. The most commonly used research methods have been outlined and their strengths and limitations have been discussed. Case studies and interactive exercises have been used throughout and you have been encouraged to work through the book as an active participant.

You have had an opportunity to get a glimpse behind the scenes at how knowledge is produced and to appreciate that there are many different types of knowledge. It is not uncommon for students to come to the research component of their studies feeling that research is an intimidating, technical process that should be left to other disciplines. Indeed, some may feel that, as one of my students phrased it, research is about 'white men in white coats'. A key message of the book is that such images should be challenged, particularly as they can become self-fulfilling. You have been invited to consider a wide range of approaches to research, including designs that incorporate social work values. You have been introduced to new tools that can enable you to challenge your own thinking and the thinking of others and to critically engage with the research literature rather than taking it at face value.

Another of the key messages is that, although the research process has different stages, you will find yourself moving between several stages at any one time as your project develops. Each stage is a building block, which requires you to re-evaluate earlier phases in the light of new information. This mirrors social work practice and the skills you develop will be valuable in your future career.

The government is introducing structures to recognise and support the status of more experienced practitioners and promoting access to postgraduate study. Advanced study will involve an increased emphasis on research skills, whether critically appraising the research of others or engaging in research yourself.

For all practitioners, there will be an increasing expectation that we will be able to provide evidence to support the decisions that we make and the interventions that we choose. The research skills that you have already developed have begun to prepare you for this challenge, but do consider how postgraduate study can take this further.

Completing your degree is an important staging post, but your professional development should not stop at that point. As a condition of continuing your registration as a social worker with the General Social Care Council, you are required to demonstrate at least 90 hours (15 days) of professional development study over a three-year period. This would be easily satisfied by most forms of post-qualifying (PQ) study but the guidelines are sufficiently broad to promote a range of learning activities. For example, the increasing profile of research digests in professional publications as well as in academic journals has made professional updating easier and more accessible.

Social care is a quickly changing environment shaped by a range of different influences, including political considerations, public perceptions and resource constraints. The evidence base for social work is constantly growing, both within social work and neighbouring disciplines. At least some of you will be research active and will contribute towards this body of knowledge. As a profession, we need to take the initiative to seek and secure research evidence for our work and to make the case for our interventions. Otherwise, we abdicate responsibility to other disciplines and decision-makers who may not share the values and priorities of social work (Campbell-King, 2008).

Glossary

Accidental sampling A lesser used term for *convenience sampling*.

Action research An approach that challenges the traditional conception of the researcher as separate from the real world. It is associated with smaller-scale research projects that seek to address real-world problems, particularly among practitioners who want to improve practice. Rather than a specific research method, it is more an approach to research that stresses the importance of links with real-world problems and a belief that research should serve practical ends.

Boolean operators Specific codes used during electronic literature searches to manipulate your search terms to achieve the best results.

Case study A detailed investigation of a single or small numbers of cases, e.g. an organisation, individual or event. Rather than a research method, it is more a focus of study in which a variety *of research methods* can be used.

Content analysis A way of analysing documents and texts. As a quantitative approach, it analyses text by measuring the frequency and prominence of specific words or phrases, e.g. stigmatising terms used in newspaper articles about asylum seekers. Qualitative versions are also used.

Convenience sampling A form of sampling in which you select your participants on the basis of what is immediately available. This is the least well regarded of sampling strategies.

Data The information that you are going to collect in order to answer your research question. In qualitative research, it is the words used by your participants or contained in texts whereas in quantitative research, data are in numerical form.

Epistemology The study of knowledge. Every approach to research has underlying assumptions about the nature of knowledge and the social world which is referred to as an *epistemological position*. Common approaches are *positivism* (quantitative research) and *interpretivism* (qualitative research).

Focus group A group of individuals selected to provide their opinions on a defined subject, facilitated by a moderator who aims to create an open and relaxed environment and promote interaction between participants.

Grounded theory An approach to research that emphasises the importance of generating new concepts and theoretical frameworks from data. Data collection and analysis happen alongside one another and data is analysed as it is collected in a continuous process. This continues until new data do not provide any new insights, the point known as theoretical saturation. Key theorists include Glaser, Strauss and Corbin.

Hypothesis   Refers to a theoretical statement about the relationship between two or more variables that predicts an expected outcome. It may be derived from your reading of the literature, a theory or your own observations and experience and must be able to be tested.

Interpretivism   A broad term to describe a range of *epistemological* approaches that challenge the traditional scientific approach of *positivism*. Interpretivism argues that the research methods of the natural sciences are inappropriate to study social phenomena because they do not take into account the viewpoints of the social actors involved.

Interview schedule   A list of questions that you intend to ask in an interview. The equivalent for *focus groups* is called a *discussion guide*.

Literature review   A comprehensive summary and critical appraisal of the literature that is relevant to your research topic. It presents the reader with what is already known in this field and identifies traditional and current controversies as well as weaknesses and gaps in the field.

Literature search   Refers to the process of identifying texts that are appropriate using electronic or manual searches. Often treated as if it was synonymous with *literature review*.

Methodology   Refers to the totality of how you are going to undertake your research. It consists of the *research approach* that you will use and the specific *research methods* you will choose.

Multi-stage cluster sampling   A sampling strategy that can be used when a sample is geographically spread. Cluster sampling enables you to group together potential participants and randomly select different sites.

Operationalisation   The process of how to convert an abstract concept into a quantifiable measure through deciding which indicators to use when measuring a particular *variable*.

Participants   Replaces the outmoded term 'research subjects' because the latter term suggests that people involved in research should have a passive role in a process to which they are 'subjected'. The term 'participants' suggests a more active and equal role, in which participation is informed and freely chosen.

Participatory action research (PAR)   A form of *action research* that is committed to the involvement of those who are most affected by the issues being studied. It challenges the traditional power imbalance between the researcher as 'expert' and research participant as 'passive subject' and is highly compatible with anti-discriminatory and anti-oppressive practice.

Population   Refers to the total group of people or other units, e.g. documents, that are being researched.

Positivism   A view of knowledge in which the methods of the traditional natural sciences are seen as appropriate to the study of social reality. It stresses objectivity and seeks to establish causal relationships. Founded by the sociologist Auguste Comte, it has been influential in quantitative social research.

Probability or random sampling   Uses mathematical techniques based upon probability theory to select research participants who are representative of the overall population. It is the most commonly used sampling approach used in questionnaire research and randomisation increases the likelihood that the results will be generalisable to a wider population. It has many forms, including *simple random sampling*, *simple stratified sampling* and *multi-stage cluster sampling*.

Purposive sampling (otherwise known as judgemental sampling)   A popular approach used in qualitative research where participants are chosen because they possess relevant characteristics for the research questions, such as particular experience or knowledge. The aim is to produce theoretical and interesting data rather than statistically generalisable findings.

Qualitative research   Tends to emphasise words as data, such as the words of participants in an interview or written data from documents. Rather than seeking to develop specific testable hypotheses, qualitative research seeks to explain the meaning of social phenomena through exploring the ways in which individuals understand their social worlds.

Quantitative research   Tends to emphasise quantification and measurement, which can be analysed using statistical tests to establish causal relationships between variables. Tends to be influenced by *positivism* as a traditional scientific model, which emphasises 'objectivity' by seeking to remove the values and attitudes of the researcher from the study. Sampling issues are particularly important because of the emphasis on being able to create statistical generalisations that are applicable to the wider population.

Quota sampling   Is a procedure in which the researcher decides to research groups or quotas of people from specific subsections of the total population. Common categories are demographic such as age, gender and ethnicity, but they could be related to the research topic.

Randomised controlled trial (RCT)   A classical experimental design, in which participants are randomly assigned to one of two groups: an experimental group and a control group. The experimental group receives the intervention while the control group does not, and the effects are then measured in each group.

Reliability   A measure of how consistent or stable a particular measure is.

Research approach   Refers to your overall view of research. A key distinction is between *quantitative* and *qualitative research* approaches. *Quantitative research* uses information in numerical form and has traditionally been influenced by a scientific worldview, most usually *positivism*. It stresses objectivity and seeks causal explanations. *Qualitative research* tends to use data in the form of words and seeks to explain the meaning of social phenomena through understanding the ways in which individuals make sense of their social worlds.

Research method   Refers to the practical ways that you are going to use to collect your data. The four most commonly used methods in student research are interviews, questionnaires, focus groups and documentary analysis. Each method has a separate chapter.

Sampling   Refers to the process of selecting the participants (or other data sources, e.g. documents) that will be involved in your study. Your *sample* (the selection of people or other data sources) is chosen from the total possible data sources, known as the *population*. *Sample* refers to the segment of the population that is selected for the research study. *Sampling frame* refers to a list of all members of the population being researched, e.g. a list of all students at a university or every social worker on the GSCC register.

Simple random sampling   The most basic form *of random sampling* in which cases are selected randomly. Each unit of the population has an equal chance of being included in the sample and this method eliminates human bias.

Simple stratified sampling   Recognises the different strata in a population and aims to select a representative sample by ensuring each section is appropriately represented.

Snowball sampling   A technique where the researcher selects a small number of participants and asks them to recommend other suitable people who may be willing to participate in the study. This is appropriate when participants are difficult to identify and contact, such as sex workers or people who are homeless.

Surveys   Used to study large groups or populations, usually using a standardised, quantitative approach to identify beliefs, attitudes, behaviour and other characteristics. *Questionnaires* form a key research method for collecting survey data, but surveys can use a range of methods, such as highly structured, face-to-face or telephone interviews.

Systematic review A form of literature review that uses an explicit and transparent set of formal protocols that seek to minimise the chances of systematic bias and error. This is usually commissioned by governmental or national bodies such as the Social Care Institute for Excellence (SCIE) in order to provide guidance about specific areas of practice and does not usually form part of undergraduate research projects.

Systematic sampling A variation of the *simple random sample* in which cases are selected in a systematic way, e.g. choosing every tenth case.

Thematic analysis A popular method for analysing qualitative data by identifying patterns of meaning. It is a versatile and flexible approach that can be used with a range of different qualitative approaches.

Theoretical sampling A type of non-probability sampling in which the sample is chosen because it is anticipated to illustrate and lead to further refinement of a theoretical issue. Developed as part of *grounded theory*, it has been argued that it is effectively synonymous with *purposive sampling*. Rather than predetermine the number of participants, researchers will carry on interviewing participants until 'saturation' has been achieved, where no significantly new data is being produced and the themes have been exhausted.

Validity Refers to whether what we are measuring is what we think we are measuring.

Variables Attributes that can take on different values with different cases and could include your participants' attitudes, beliefs, behaviour, knowledge or some other characteristic.

References

Abt Associates (2001) *National evaluation of family support programs – Volume B research studies: Final report*. Cambridge, MA. **www.abtassoc.com/reports/NEFSP-VolB.pdf**.

Alston, M and Bowles, W (1998) *Research for social workers*. St Leonard, NSW: Allen & Unwin.

Andersen, ML and Taylor, HF (2005) *Sociology: Understanding a diverse society*. Belmont, CA: Thomson Wadsworth.

Andrews, M, Squire, C and Tamboukou, M (eds) (2008) *Doing narrative research*. London: Sage.

Andrews, M, Day Sclater, S, Rustin, M, Squire, C and Treacher, A (eds) (2004) *Uses of narrative*. New Brunswick, NJ: Transition.

Arksey, H and Knight, P (1999) *Interviewing for social scientists: An introductory resource with examples*. London: Sage.

Atkinson, JM and Heritage, J (1984) *Structures of social action: Studies in conversation analysis*. Cambridge: Cambridge University Press.

Barbour, RS and Kitzinger, J (1999) *Developing focus group research: Politics, theory and practice*. London: Sage.

Barthes, R (1972) *Mythologies*. New York: Hill & Wang.

Becker, H (1986) *Writing for social scientists: How to start and finish your thesis, book or article*. Chicago, IL: University of Chicago Press.

Becker, H (2007) *Writing for social scientists: How to start and finish your thesis, book or article*. 2nd edition, Chicago, IL: University of Chicago Press.

Berelson, B (1952) *Content analysis in communication research*. New York: Free Press.

Bhaskar, R (1978) *A realist theory of science*. 2nd edition. Atlantic Highlands, NJ: Humanities Press.

Bhaskar, R (1979) *The possibility of naturalism: A philosophical critique of the contemporary human sciences*. Brighton: Harvester.

Bhasker, R (1990) *Harré and his critics*. Oxford: Blackwell.

Biehal, N (2005) Working with adolescents at risk of out of home care: the effectiveness of specialist teams. *Children and Youth Services Review*, 27 (9): 1045–59.

Biehal, N (2008) Preventive services for adolescents: exploring the process of change. *British Journal of Social Work*, 38 (3): 444–61.

Bottomore, TB and Rubel, M (1963) *Karl Marx: Selected writings in sociology and social philosophy.* Harmondsworth: Penguin.

Boyatzis, RE (1998) *Transforming qualitative information: Thematic analysis and code development.* Thousand Oaks, CA: Sage.

Braun, V and Clarke, V (2006) Using thematic analysis in psychology. *Qualitative Research in Psychology,* 3: 77–101.

Brink P (1991) Issues of reliability and validity. In J Morse (ed) *Qualitative nursing research: A contemporary dialogue.* London, Sage.

Bryman, A (2008) *Social research methods.* 3rd edition. Oxford: Oxford University Press.

Campbell-King, I (2008) The challenge for newly-qualified social workers. Unpublished conference paper, London South Bank University, July.

Clements, S and Foster, N (2008) Newspaper reporting on schizophrenia: A content analysis of five national newspapers at two time points. *Schizophrenia Research,* 98: 178–83.

Crossley, M (2000) *Introducing narrative psychology: Self, trauma and construction of meaning.* Buckingham: Open University Press.

Crossley, M (2007) Narrative analysis. In E Lyons and A Coyle (eds) *Qualitative data analysis in psychology.* London: Sage.

Crossley, M and Crossley, N (2001) Patient voices, social movements and the habitus: How psychiatric survivors 'speak out'. *Social Science and Medicine,* 52: 1477–89.

Crotty, M (1998) *The foundations of social research: Meaning and perspectives in the research process.* London: Sage.

Culley, L, Hudson, N and Rapport, F (2007) Using focus groups with minority ethnic communities: Researching infertility in British South Asian communities. *Qualitative Health Research,* 17: 102–12.

Curtis, EA and Redmond, R (2007) Focus groups in nursing research. *Nurse Researcher,* 14(2): 25–37.

David, M (2006) Editor's introduction. In *Case study research: Sage benchmarks in social research methods,* Vol. 1. London: Sage.

Davies, M (1997) Shattered assumptions: Time and the experience of long-term HIV positivity. *Social Science and Medicine,* 44: 561–71.

Davies, MB (2007) *Doing a successful research project: Using qualitative or quantitative methods.* Basingstoke: Palgrave Macmillan.

Day, C, Carey, M and Surgenor, T (2006) Children's key concerns: piloting a qualitative approach to understanding their experience of mental health care. *Clinical Child Psychology and Psychiatry,* 11: 139.

De Vaus, DA (2002) *Surveys in social research,* 5th edition. London: Routledge.

Delamont, S, Atkinson, P, Parry, O (2004) *Supervising the PhD: A guide to success,* 2nd edition. Buckingham: Open University Press.

Denscombe, M (2007) *The good research guide for small-scale social research projects,* 3rd edition. Buckingham: Open University Press.

Department of Health (2005) *Research governance framework for health and social care,* 2nd edition. London: DoH.

Dunleavy, P (2003) *Authoring a PhD: How to plan, draft, write and finish a doctoral thesis or dissertation*. Basingstoke: Palgrave Macmillan.

Elliott, J (2005) *Using narrative in social research: Qualitative and quantitative approaches*. London: Sage.

Farquhar, C (with Das, R) (1999) Are focus groups suitable for sensitive topics? In RS Barbour and J Kitzinger (eds) *Developing focus group research: Politics, theory and practice*. London: Sage.

Finch, J (1987) The vignette technique in survey research. *Sociology*, 21: 105–14.

Fink, A (2005) *Conducting research literature reviews: From the internet to paper*. 2nd edition. Thousand Oaks, CA: Sage.

Fink, A (2006) *How to conduct surveys: A step-by-step guide*. 3rd edition. Thousand Oaks, CA: Sage.

Forrester, D, Kershaw, S, Moss, H and Hughes, L (2008) Communication skills in child protection: how do social workers talk to parents? *Child and family social work*, 13: 41–51.

Forrester, D, McCambridge, J, Waissbein, C, Emlyn-Jones, R and Rollnick, R (2008) Child risk and parental resistance: can motivational interviewing improve the practice of child and family social workers in working with parental alcohol misuse? *British Journal of Social Work*, 38(7): 1302–19.

Frank, A (1995) *The wounded storyteller: Body, illness and ethics*. Chicago, IL: University of Chicago Press.

Free, C, White, P, Shipman, C and Dale, J (1999) Access to and use of out-of-hours services by members of Vietnamese community groups in South London: A focus group study. *Family Practice*, 16(4): 369–74.

Ghate, D, Shaw, C and Hazel, N (2000) *Fathers and family centres: Engaging fathers in preventive services*. York: Joseph Rowntree Foundation.

Gibbs, GR (2007) *Analysing qualitative data*. London: Sage.

Giddens, A (1993) *New rules of sociological method: A positive critique of interpretative sociologies*. 2nd edition. Cambridge: Polity Press.

Giddens, A (2006) *Sociology*, 5th edition. Cambridge: Polity Press.

Glaser, B and Strauss, A (1967) *The discovery of grounded theory*. Chicago, IL: Aldine.

Gray, DE (2004) *Doing research in the real world*. London: Sage.

Green, J and Hart, L (1999) The impact of context on data. In RS Barbour and J Kitzinger (eds), *Developing focus group research: Politics, theory and practice*. London: Sage.

Gubrium, JF and Holstein, JA (2009) *Analysing narrative reality*. Thousand Oaks, CA: Sage.

Happel, B (2007) Focus groups in nursing research: an appropriate method or the latest fad? *Nurse Researcher*, 14(2): 18–24.

Hart, C (2001) *Doing a literature search: A comprehensive guide for the social sciences*. London: Sage.

Hek, G and Moule, P (2006) *Making sense of research: An introduction for health and social care practitioners*. London: Sage.

Heron, J and Reason, P (2006) The practice of co-operative inquiry: research 'with' rather than 'on' people. In P Reason and H Bradbury (eds) *Handbook of action research*. London: Sage.

Hertel, B (1976) Minimising error variance introduced by missing data routes in survey analysis. *Sociological Methods and Research*, 4: 459–74.

Hinchman, LP and Hinchman, SK (1997) Introduction. In LP Hinchman and SK Hinchman (eds) *Memory, identity, community: The idea of narrative in the human sciences.* New York: State University of New York.

Huberman, M and Miles, M (1998) Data management and analysis methods. In N Denzin and Y Lincoln (eds.) *Collecting and interpreting qualitative materials.* London: Sage.

Humphries, B (2008) *Social work research for social justice.* Basingstoke: Palgrave Macmillan.

Janis, IL (1982) *Groupthink.* 2nd edition. Boston, MA: Houghton Mufflin.

Kirby, S and McKenna, K (1989) *Experience, research, social change: Methods from the margins.* Toronto: Garamond.

Kitzinger, J (1994) The methodology of focus groups: the importance of interaction between research participants. *Sociology of Health and Illness*, 16(1): 103–21.

Kratochwill, TR, McDonald, L, Levin, JR, Young Bear-Tibbetts, H, and Demaray, MK (2004) Families and schools together: An experimental analysis of a parent-mediated multi-family group program for American Indian children. *Journal of School Psychology*, 42: 359–83.

Krueger, RA (1994). *Focus groups: A practical guide for applied research.* Thousand Oaks, CA: Sage.

Krueger, RA and Casey, MA (2000) *Focus groups.* 3rd edition. Thousand Oaks, CA: Sage.

Kvale, S (1996) *Interviews: An introduction to qualitative research interviewing.* London: Sage.

Labov, W and Waletsky, J (1967) Narrative analysis: oral versions of personal experience. In J Helms (ed) *Essays in the Verbal and Visual Arts.* Seattle, WA: University of Washington.

Layder, D (1993) *New strategies in social research.* Cambridge: Polity Press.

Leki, I (1998) *Academic writing: Exploring processes and strategies.* Cambridge: Cambridge University Press.

Lincoln, YS and Guba, EG (1985) *Naturalistic inquiry.* London: Sage.

Ludema, JD, Cooperrider, DL and Barrett, FJ (2006) Appreciative inquiry: The power of the unconditional positive question. In P Reason and H Bradbury (eds) *Handbook of action research.* London: Sage.

Lyons, E and Coyle, A (2007) *Qualitative data analysis in psychology.* London: Sage.

McCulloch, G (2004) *Documentary research in education, history and the social sciences.* London: Routledge Falmer.

Macdonald, J (2003) *Using systematic reviews to improve social care*, SCIE Report No. 4. London: Social Care Institute for Excellence.

McDonald, L, Moberg, DP, Brown, R, Rodriguez-Espiricueta, I, Flores, N, Burke, MP, et al. (2006) After-school multifamily groups: A randomized controlled trial involving low-income, urban, Latino children. *Children and Schools*, 18: 25–34.

Mair, M (1989) *Between psychology and psychotherapy.* London: Routledge.

Mason, J (2002) *Qualitative researching.* 2nd edition. London: Sage.

Maxwell, JA (1996) *Qualitative research design: An interactive approach.* Thousand Oaks, CA: Sage.

Merton, RK, Fiske, M and Kendall, P (1990) *The focused interview*. 2nd edition. New York: Free Press.

Michell, L (1999) Combining focus groups and interviews: telling how it is, telling how it feels. In RS Barbour and J Kitzinger (eds), *Developing focus group research*. London: Sage.

Miles, MB and Huberman, AM (1994) *Qualitative data analysis: An expanded sourcebook*. 2nd edition. London: Sage.

Morgan, DL (ed) (1993) *Successful focus groups: Advancing the state of the art*. London: Sage.

Morgan, DL (1997) *Focus groups as qualitative research*. 2nd edition. London: Sage.

Morgan, DL (1998) *Planning focus groups*. Thousand Oaks, CA: Sage.

Nardi, PM (2006) *Doing survey research: A guide to quantitative methods*. Boston, MA: Allyn & Bacon.

Neuman, WL (2006) *Basics of social research: Qualitative and quantitative approaches*. 2nd edition. Boston, MA: Allyn & Bacon.

O'Leary, Z (2004) *The essential guide to doing research*. London: Sage.

Owen, S (2001) The practical, methodological and ethical dilemmas of conducting focus groups with vulnerable clients. *Journal of Advanced Nursing*, 36(5): 652–8.

Parker, I (1992) *Discourse dynamics: Critical analysis for social and individual psychology*. London: Routledge.

Parton, N (2004) From Maria Colwell to Victoria Climbié: Reflections on public inquires into child abuse a generation apart. *Child Abuse Review*, 13: 80–94.

Payne, G and Payne, J (2004) *Key concepts in social research*. London: Sage.

Philo, G (ed) (1996) *Media and mental distress*. Harlow: Longman.

Plano Clarke, VL and Cresswell, JW (2008) *The mixed methods reader*. London: Sage.

Potter, J and Wetherell, M (1987) *Discourse and social psychology: Beyond attitudes and behaviour*. London: Sage.

Quality Assurance Agency for Higher Education (QAA) (2008) *Subject Benchmark Statement – Social Work*. Online at: **www.qaa.ac.uk/academicinfrastructure/benchmark/statements/social-work 08.asp.**

Riessman, C (1993) *Narrative analysis*. London: Sage.

Riessman, C (2007) *Narrative methods for the human sciences*. London: Sage.

Robinson, FP (1970) *Effective study*. 4th edition. New York: Harper and Row.

Robson, C (2002) *Real world research: A resource for social scientists and practitioner-researchers*. 2nd edition. Oxford: Blackwell.

Rustin, M (2000) Reflections on the biographical turn in the social sciences. In P Chamberlayne, J Bornat and T Wengraf (eds), *The turn to biographical methods in social science*. London: Routledge.

Sarbin, TR (1986) *Narrative psychology: The storied nature of human conduct*. Westport, CT: Praeger.

Sarantakos, S (2005) *Social research*. 3rd edition. Basingstoke: Palgrave Macmillan.

Saussure, F de (1983) *Course in general linguistics*. London: Duckworth.

Schneider, JK, Schneider, J and Lorenz, R (2005) Creating user-friendly databases with Microsoft Access. *Nurse Researcher*, 13(1): 57–75.

Scott, J (1990) *A matter of record: Documentary sources in social research.* Cambridge: Polity Press.

Scottish Executive (2003) *Focus groups with minority ethnic communities.* Edinburgh: The Stationery Office.

Scourfield, J (2001) Interviewing interviewers and knowing about knowledge. In I Shaw and N Gould (eds) *Qualitative research in social work.* London: Sage.

Scourfield, J (2006) The challenge of engaging fathers in the child protection process. *Critical Social Policy*, 26: 440–9.

Sharp, J (2009) *Success with your education research project.* Exeter: Learning Matters.

Silverman, D (2001) *Interpreting qualitative data*. 2nd edition. London: Sage.

Silverman, D (2005) *Doing qualitative research*. 2nd edition. London: Sage.

Sim, J (1998) Collecting and analysing qualitative data: issues raised by the focus group. *Journal of Advanced Nursing*, 28(2): 345–52.

Smith, J (2002) Department of Health Press Release Reference 2002/0241. Online at: **www.info. doh.gov.uk/intpress.nsf/page/2002-0241/?OpenDocument**.

Squire, C, Andrews, M and Tamboukou, M (2008) What is narrative research? In M Andrews, C Squire and M Tamboukou (eds) *Doing narrative research.* London: Sage.

Strauss, A and Corbin, J (1998) *Basics of qualitative research: Techniques and procedures for developing grounded theory*. London: Sage.

Thierfelder, C, Tanner, M and Bodiang, C (2005) Female genital mutilation in the context of migration: Experience of African women with the Swiss health care system. *European Journal of Public Health*, 15(1): 86–90.

Thurlow-Brown, N (1988) The Curate's Egg. Unpublished conference paper, North East Essex Mental Health Trust.

Vaughn, S, Schumm, JS and Sinagub, J (1996) *Focus group interviews in education and psychology*. Thousand Oaks, CA: Sage.

Vissandjée, B, Abdool, S and Dupéré, S (2002) Focus groups in rural Gujarat, India: A modified approach. *Qualitative Health Research*, 12(6): 826–43.

Walliman, N (2006) *Social research methods*. London: Sage.

Wilks, T (2004) The use of vignettes in qualitative research into social work values. *Qualitative Social Work*, 3(1): 78–87.

Yin, R (2003) *Case study research: Design and methods*. 3rd edition. London: Sage.

Zeller, R (1993) Focus group research on sensitive topics: Setting the agenda without setting the agenda. In DL Morgan (ed) *Successful focus groups: Advancing the state of the art*. London: Sage.

Index

Added to the page number 'f' denotes a figure and 'g' denotes the glossary.